A SKILLS-BASED SHORT COURSE

STARTER

Series editor: Philip Prowse

DAVID BOWKER • PATRICIA LODGE

Heinemann English Language Teaching
A division of Reed Educational and Professional Publishing Limited
Halley Court, Jordan Hill, Oxford OX2 8EJ

OXFORD MADRID FLORENCE ATHENS PRAGUE
SÃO PAULO MEXICO CITY CHICAGO
PORTSMOUTH (NH) TOKYO SINGAPORE
KUALA LUMPUR MELBOURNE AUCKLAND
JOHANNESBURG IBADAN GABORONE

ISBN 0 435 28272 7

First published 1997

Designed by Ken Vail Graphic Design
Cover design by Threefold Design
Cover photograph by Frank Orel/Tony Stone Images

Illustrated by: Archer Art (Ross), Paul Collicutt, Richard Duszczak, Simon Girling and Associates (Mike Lacey, Alex Pang), Tim Kahane, Joanne Makin, Gillian Martin, John Plumb, Mike Whelan, Ken Vail Graphic Design (Matthew Clubb, Graeme Morris).

The authors and publishers would like to thank the following for permission to reproduce their photographs: Action Plus p10(bc), 61(bc); The Anthony Blake Photo Library p32(t), (bc), (br), p34; Bubbles Photo Library p61(br); Gerrit Buntrock p81; Cephas Picture Library p13(t); John Cleare/Mountain Camera Picture Library p49; Collections p10(tc), (bl); Mary Evans Picture Library Ltd p45(tl); The Image Bank p10(tr), (mr), (br), p13(ml), p40(ml); The Kobal Collection Ltd p45(tr), (bl); Lorenz Books/Anness Publishing p32(bl); NHPA p13(mr), (br); Pictor International Ltd p13(tr), (bl), p36, p59(tl), (bl), p78; Powerstock Photo Library p13(tl); p40(tr), p52, p53(tl), p70, p88; Rex Features Ltd p53(b), p59(br), p61(bl); Tony Stone Images p10(mc), (bc), p39, p40(mr), (mc), p59(tr), p61(bc); Trip p53(tr); Zefa Pictures Ltd p10(ml), p40(br).

We would also like to thank River Island Clothing Company Limited – Oxford Branch for their help with location photography.

Commissioned photography by Sue Baker p6, p7, p24, p26.

Picture Research by Mandy Twells

Printed in Scotland by Cambus Litho

97 98 99 00 01 10 9 8 7 6 5 4 3 2 1

The authors and publishers would like to thank the following for permission to reproduce their material: 'What a Wonderful World' words and music by Bob Thiele and George D Weiss © 1967 by Range Road Music Inc. Quartet Music Co Inc and Abilene Music Inc. Lyric reproduction by permission of Carlin Music Corp – UK administrator; 'Homeward Bound' © Paul Simon (BMI)/Pattern Music Ltd 1966.

The authors would like to thank Philip Prowse.

The series editor and the authors would like to thank Catherine Smith and Celia Bingham for their professionalism, dedication and good humour.

The publishers would like to thank Sam Pinniger, Robert Ritchie, Lydia Trapnell and St Joseph's Hall, Oxford.

Contents

Map of the book

Unit 1
Hello!
Lesson 1 Where are you from? 6
Lesson 2 He's my brother 8
Lesson 3 What do you do? 10

Unit 2
Places
Lesson 1 What's Sydney like? 12
Lesson 2 Where's the bank? 14
Lesson 3 What's your room like? 16

Unit 3
Travel
Lesson 1 What time does it open? 18
Lesson 2 I'd like a room please 20
Lesson 3 Winter sports 22

Unit 4
Shopping
Lesson 1 What colour is it? 24
Lesson 2 Can I try it on? 26
Lesson 3 How much is it? 28

Unit 5
Food
Lesson 1 Do you like fish? 30
Lesson 2 Have you got any prawns? 32
Lesson 3 What would you like? 34

Unit 6
Body and soul
Lesson 1 She's taller than me 36
Lesson 2 What's the matter? 38
Lesson 3 What a wonderful world 40

Unit 7
Daily life
Lesson 1 When do you get up? 42
Lesson 2 Do you like swimming? 44
Lesson 3 Can you ride a motorbike? 46

Unit 8
What happened?
Lesson 1 What was your holiday like? 48
Lesson 2 The singing burglar 50
Lesson 3 When did you last write a letter? 52

Unit 9
Making arrangements
Lesson 1 What's he doing? 54
Lesson 2 What's on? 56
Lesson 3 Are you free tonight? 58

Unit 10
Taking off
Lesson 1 The news 60
Lesson 2 Homeward bound 62
Lesson 3 Travel game 64

Student B Activities 66

Practice pages 67

Map of the book

	Language focus	Vocabulary focus
Unit 1 *Hello!*		
Lesson 1 Where are you from? Introducing yourself	*to be* questions	Alphabet Countries
Lesson 2 He's my brother Your family	*to be* Possessive 's Possessive adjectives	Family
Lesson 3 What do you do? Talking about jobs	*a/an* Plurals *any questions* Present simple questions	Jobs
Unit 2 *Places*		
Lesson 1 What's Sydney like? Describing places	*What's it like?*	Adjectives
Lesson 2 Where's the bank? Finding the way	Asking for directions Giving directions Prepositions	Shops Buildings
Lesson 3 What's your room like? Describing a room	*There's a …/There are …* Prepositions of place	Rooms and furniture
Unit 3 *Travel*		
Lesson 1 What time does it open? Telling the time	Telling the time Present simple questions	Times
Lesson 2 I'd like a room please Travelling in another country	Buying a train ticket Checking into a hotel Filling in a form	Prices
Lesson 3 Winter sports A game	Review of units 1–3 *have got*	Revision
Unit 4 *Shopping*		
Lesson 1 What colour is it? Talking about clothes	Colours	Colours Clothes
Lesson 2 Can I try it on? Buying clothes	*can* for requests *too*	Clothes Colours
Lesson 3 How much is it? Shopping	*Let's …* *going to*	Shops Things to buy
Unit 5 *Food*		
Lesson 1 Do you like fish? Likes and dislikes	Present simple: *like, love, hate*	Food: meals
Lesson 2 Have you got any prawns? Dishes from different countries	Present simple: *have got, need* Countable and uncountable nouns *any*	Revision of countries Recipes
Lesson 3 What would you like? Ordering food in a restaurant	*would like* *I'll have*	The language of menus

	Language focus	Vocabulary focus
Unit 6 *Body and soul*		
Lesson 1 She's taller than me Describing and comparing people	Comparison of adjectives	Parts of the body
Lesson 2 What's the matter? Talking about illness	Present simple negative *should*	Ailments
Lesson 3 What a wonderful world A song	Review of units 4–6	
Unit 7 *Daily life*		
Lesson 1 When do you get up? Talking about your day	Present simple for daily routines *so do I* Telling the time: *past, to*	Morning routine
Lesson 2 Do you like swimming? Sports and hobbies you like	*like -ing*	Sports Hobbies
Lesson 3 Can you ride a motorbike? Talking about ability	*can* for ability Adverbs of manner	Activities
Unit 8 *What happened?*		
Lesson 1 What was your holiday like? Talking about holidays	Past simple: *was, were* Past simple	Holidays Weather
Lesson 2 The singing burglar A story	Past simple: regular and irregular verbs Joining sentences	Crime Going on holiday
Lesson 3 When did you last write a letter? You are the detective	Times in the past	Months of the year
Unit 9 *Making arrangements*		
Lesson 1 What's he doing? Writing a postcard	Present continuous	Sports and leisure activities
Lesson 2 What's on? Making decisions	Making suggestions Saying what you want	Entertainments
Lesson 3 Are you free tonight? Inviting a friend out	Prepositions of time Present continuous for the future Making suggestions	Revision of hobbies
Unit 10 *Taking off*		
Lesson 1 The news Making a news programme	Revision of past simple Present continuous for the future	Revision: weather, sports, numbers
Lesson 2 Homeward bound A song	Revision	Revision: travel vocabulary
Lesson 3 Travel game A travel game	Revision	General revision

Unit 1 Hello!

Lesson 1 *Where are you from?*

Language focus: *to be* questions

Vocabulary focus: Alphabet
Countries

1

Hello!

2

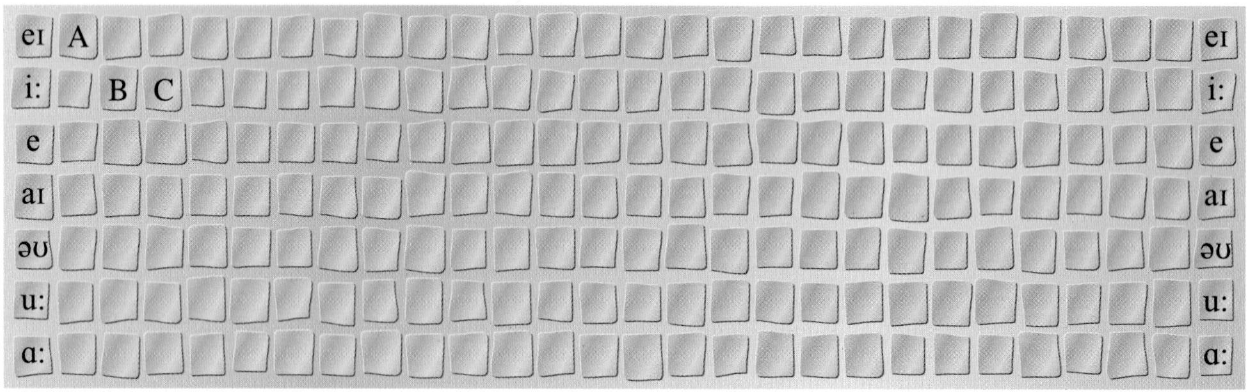

3

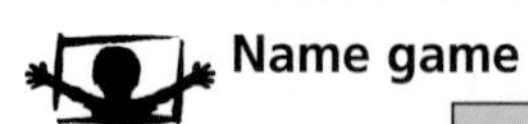

Name game

4

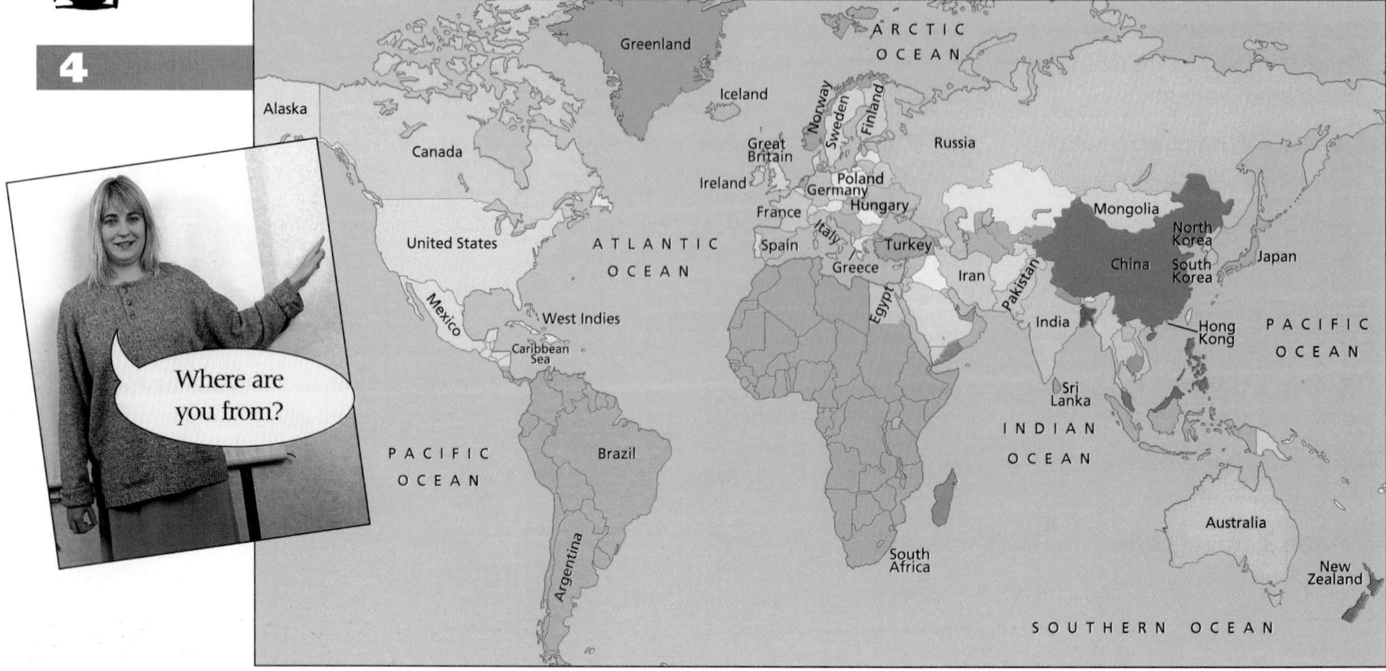

5

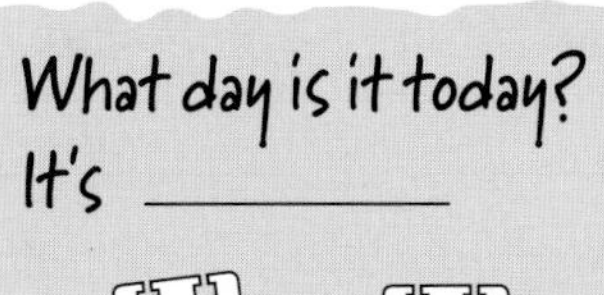

Language Summary

to be questions
Where **are you** from?
Alphabet
Countries

see practice page 67

Lesson 2 *He's my brother*

Language focus:	*to be* Possessive 's Possessive adjectives
Vocabulary focus:	Numbers 1–10 Family

1

Kevin's Family

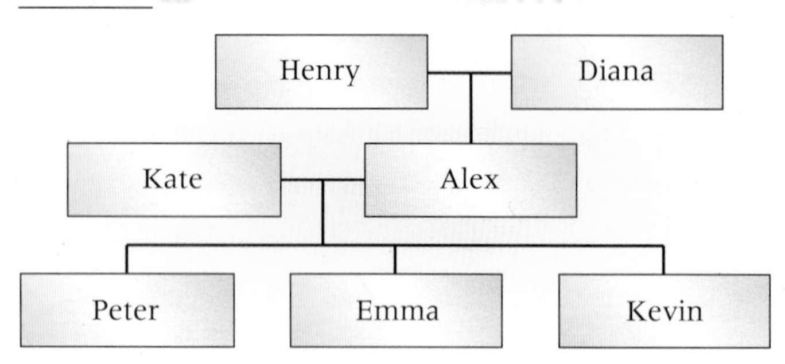

1 Henry is Kevin's *grandfather*. 2 Kate is Alex's ________.

3 Kevin is Peter's ________. 4 Emma is Kevin's ________.

5 Diana is Peter's ________. 6 Henry is Diana's ________.

7 Alex is Henry's ________. 8 Emma is Kate's ________.

9 Diana is Alex's ________. 10 Alex is Emma's ________.

11 Peter is Diana's ________. 12 Emma is Henry's ________.

2

Tom's family

Sam is Boris's grandson.

Midge is Tom's mother.

Fluffy is Sam's brother.

Tiger is Fluffy's sister.

Midge is Sam's grandmother.

Mimi is Tom's wife.

Boris is Midge's husband.

Boris is Tom's father.

Tiger is Mimi's daughter.

Tiger is Midge's granddaughter.

Fluffy is Tom's son.

Boris is Tiger's grandfather.

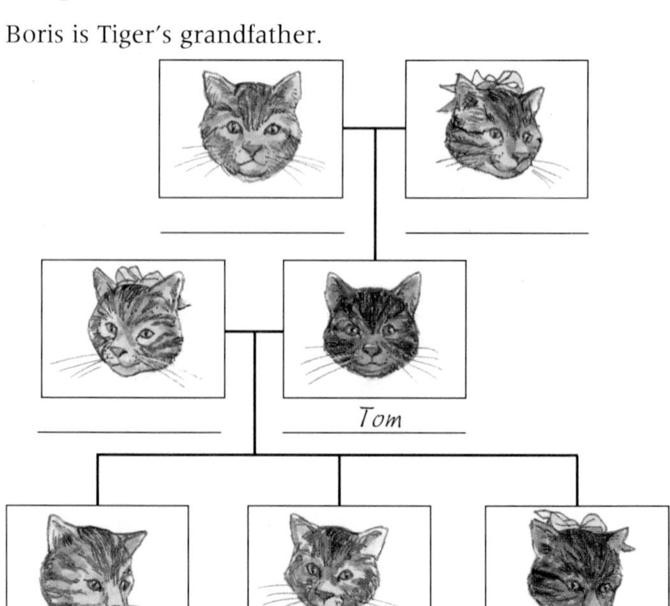

3

Stand up!

4

my your his her our their

1
Is she _______ mother ?
2
I'm _____ husband.
3
I'm _______ granddaughter.
4
She's _______ mother.
5
They're _______ parents.
PETE
6
I'm _______ sister.

5

seven ____	four ____	five ____
three ____	eight ____	two ____
nine ____	six ____	
one ____	ten ____	

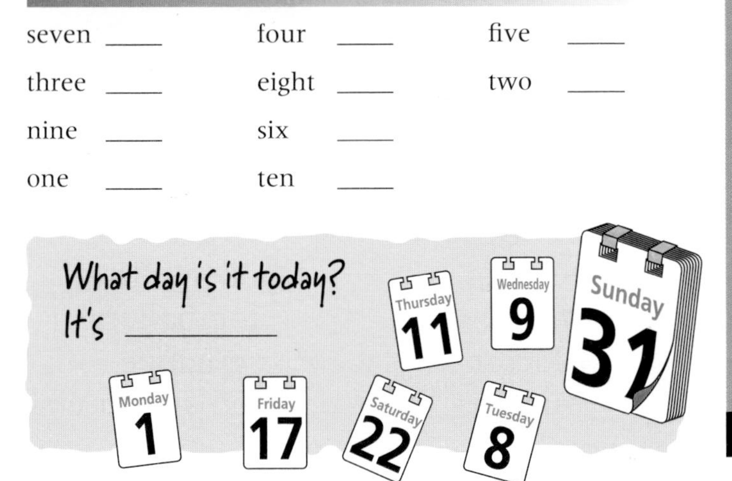

Language Summary

to be

Mimi **is** Tom's wife.
He's her husband.
Henry and Diana **are** Alex's parents.
They're Kevin's grandparents.

Possessive *'s*

Tom**'s** son

Possessive adjectives

my, your, his, her, our, their

see practice page 68

Lesson 3 *What do you do?*

Language focus: *a, an*
Plurals
any questions
Present simple questions

Vocabulary focus: Jobs

1

What does she do?
She's a doctor.
What does he do?
He's an actor.

a 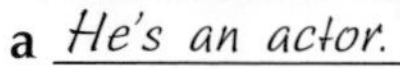 *He's an actor.*

b ____________

c ____________ d ____________

e ____________

f ____________

g ____________

h ____________

i ____________

j ____________

farmer	actor
teacher	police officer
businessman	footballers
doctor	engineer
students	shop assistant

2

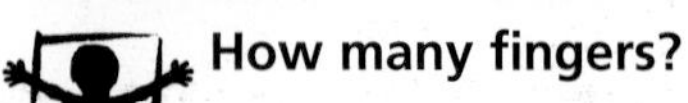 **How many fingers?**

3

Student A

		A	B
	farmers		
	birds		
	footballers		
	cats		
	doctors		
	police officers		

4

name	country	job	brothers	sisters
Melissa	______	______	___	___
______	Brazil	______	___	___
______	______	doctor	___	___
______	______	______	3	___
______	______	______	___	0
Eva	______	______	___	___
______	Spain	______	___	___

What's your name?
Where are you from?
What do you do?
Have you got any brothers/sisters?
How many?

What day is it today?
It's ______

Thursday 11 Wednesday 9 Sunday 31 Monday 1 Friday 17 Saturday 22 Tuesday 8

Language Summary

a/an
She's **a** doctor.
He's **an** actor.

plurals
They're footballer**s**.
They're business**men**.

any questions
Have you got **any** cats in your picture?

Present simple questions
What **do you/they do?**
What **does he/she do?**

see practice page 69

Lesson 1 *What's Sydney like?*

Language focus: *What's it like?*
Adjectives

1

h___ c___ w___

b___ s_____

b________ u__________

c_____ d_____

b____ n_____ q_____

d________ s____

w___ d___

2

Word mime

3

In spring it's ___________ .

In summer it's ___________ .

In autumn it's ___________ .

In winter it's ___________ .

4

New York

Sydney

Antarctica

Sahara Desert

Singapore

the Amazon Jungle

5

Match the numbers with the words.

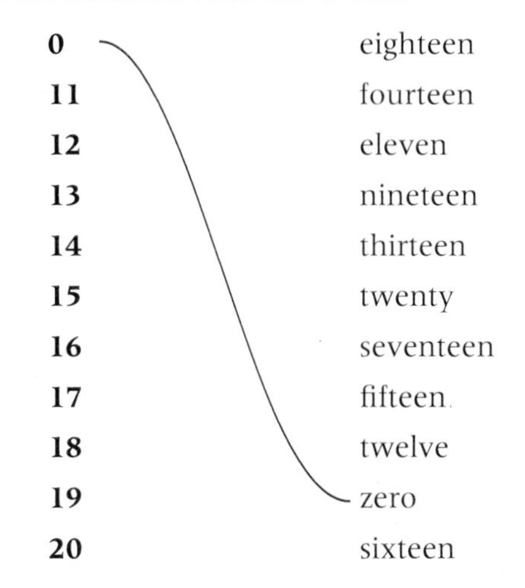

0	eighteen
11	fourteen
12	eleven
13	nineteen
14	thirteen
15	twenty
16	seventeen
17	fifteen
18	twelve
19	zero
20	sixteen

6

Bingo!

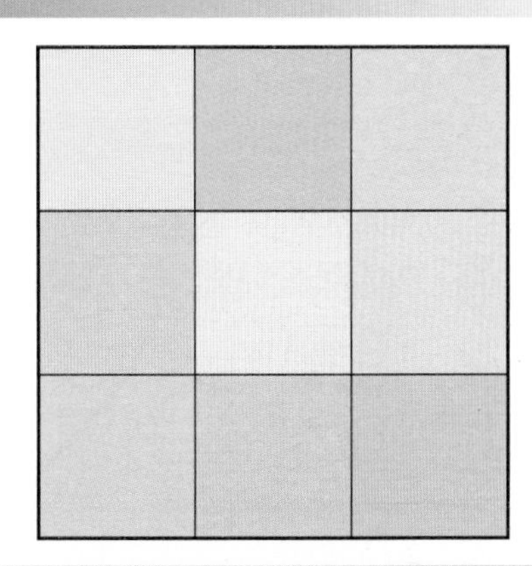

Language Summary

What's it like

What**'s** your city **like?**

Adjectives

It's **beautiful** and it's **hot** in summer.

see practice page 70

Lesson 2 *Where's the bank?*

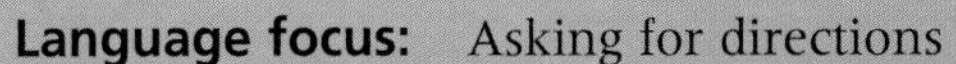

Language focus: Asking for directions
Giving directions
Prepositions

Vocabulary focus: Shops and buildings

1

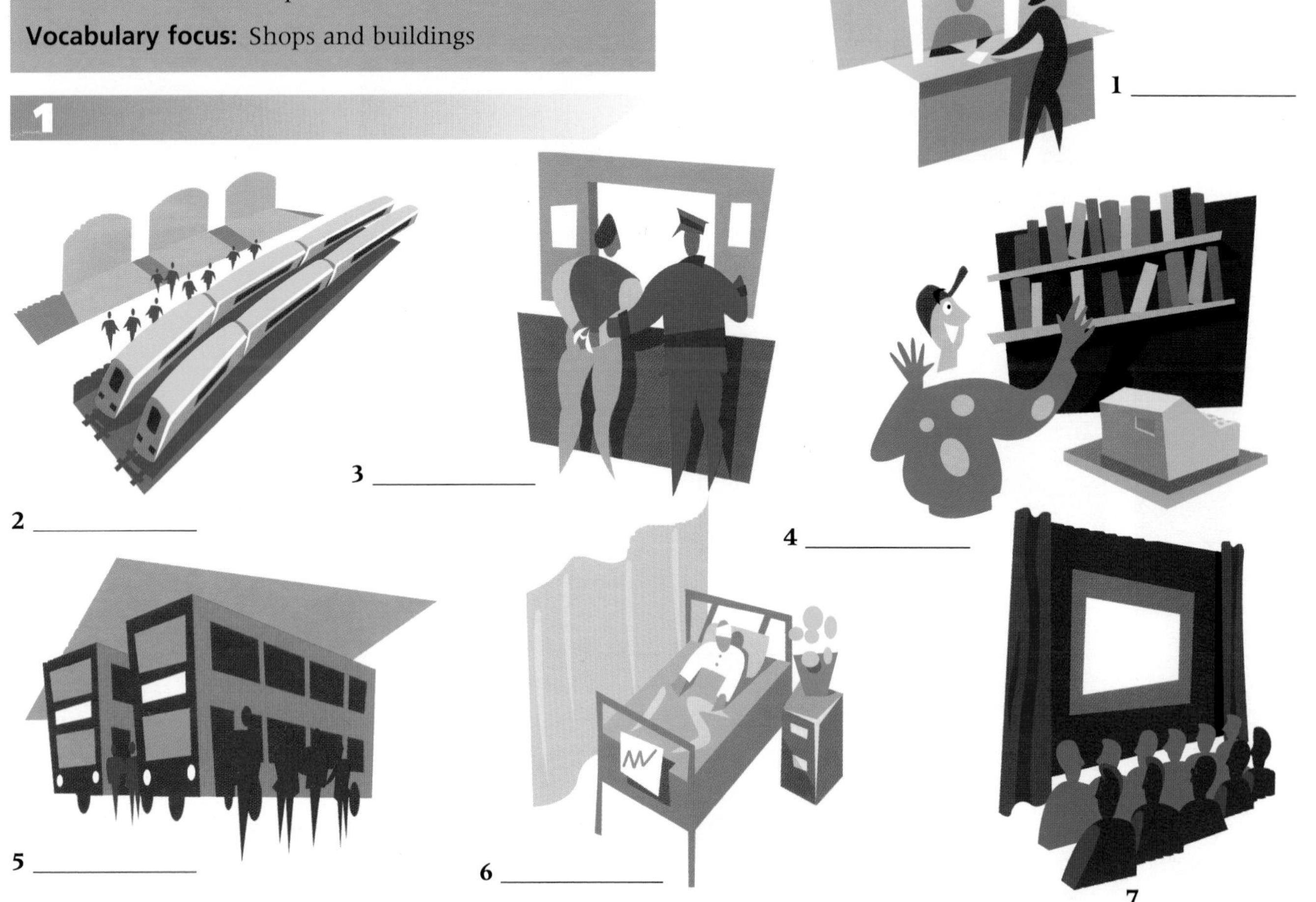

1 ____________

2 ____________

3 ____________

4 ____________

5 ____________

6 ____________

7 ____________

2

Match the words in the box to the pictures.

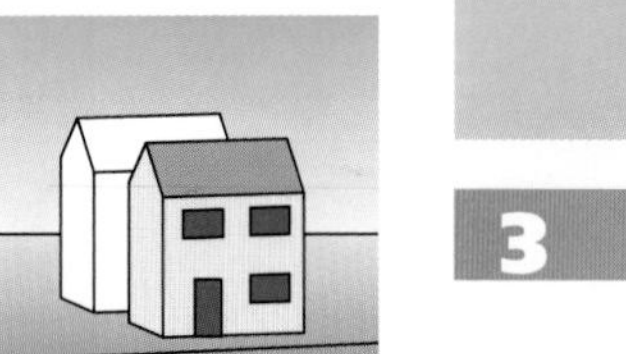

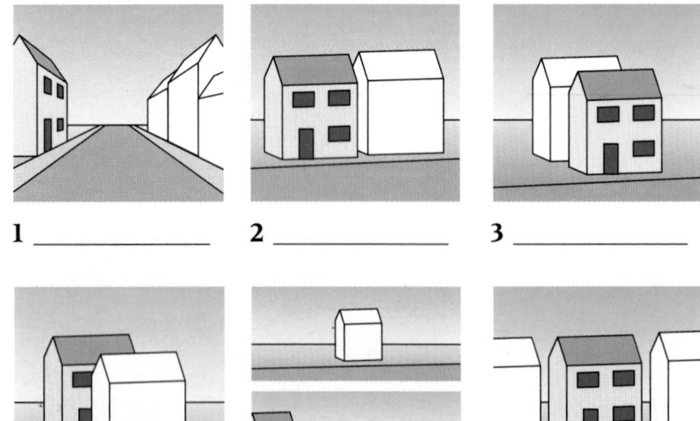

1 ____________ 2 ____________ 3 ____________

4 ____________ 5 ____________ 6 ____________

behind between in front of near next to opposite

3

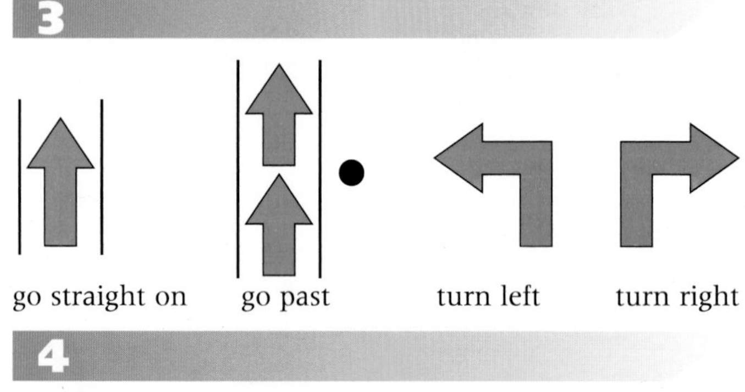

go straight on go past turn left turn right

4

Blind walking

5

Language Summary

Asking for directions

Where's the bank?

Is there a bank **near here?**

Giving directions

Go past the hotel and **turn right**.

Prepositions

It's **next to** the hotel.

see practice page 71

Lesson 3 *What's your room like?*

Language focus: *There's a …*
There are …
Prepositions of place

Vocabulary focus: Rooms and furniture

1

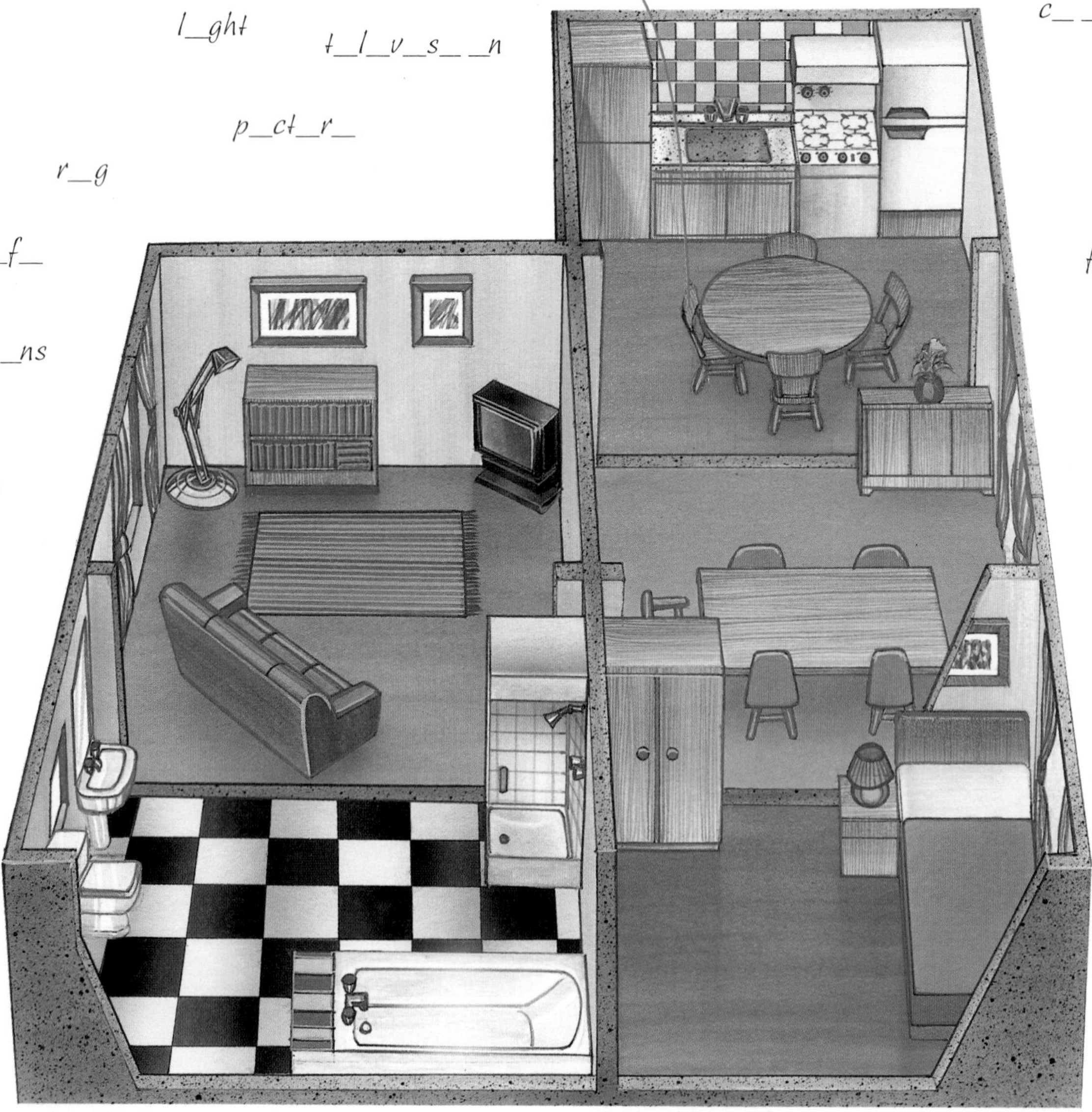

t_bl_
s_nk
c_pb_ _rd
chair
l_ght
t_l_v_s_ _n
c_ _k_r
p_ct_r_
fr_dg_
r_g
s_f_
fl_w_rs
c_rt_ _ns
c_rp_t
w_rdr_b_
b_d
b_s_n
b_th
t_ _l_t
sh_w_r

2

Touch it!

3

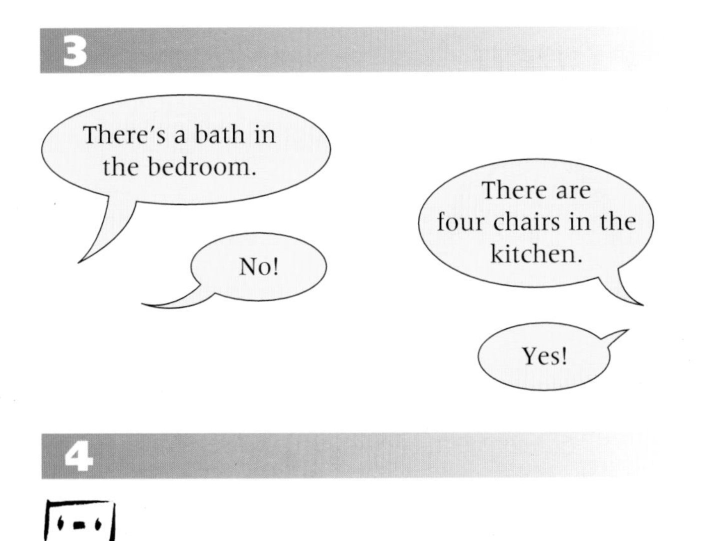

There's a bath in the bedroom.
No!
There are four chairs in the kitchen.
Yes!

4

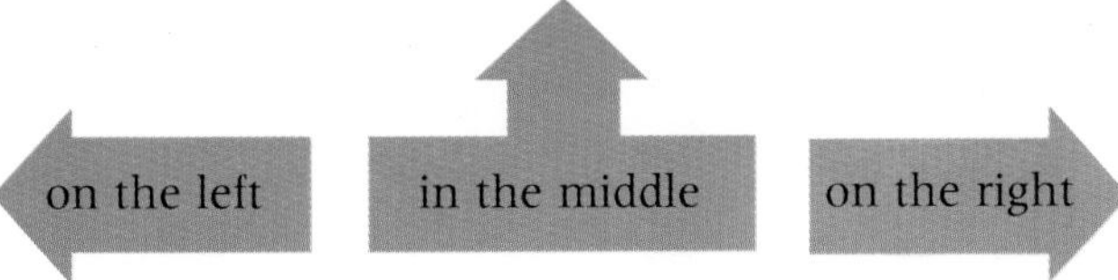

Language Summary

There is a ... / There are ...

There's a cooker in the kitchen.
There are four chairs in the dining room.

Prepositions of place

There's a picture **on** the wall.

see practice page 72

Lesson 1 *What time does it open?*

Language focus: Telling the time
Present simple questions

Vocabulary focus: Times

1

a

b
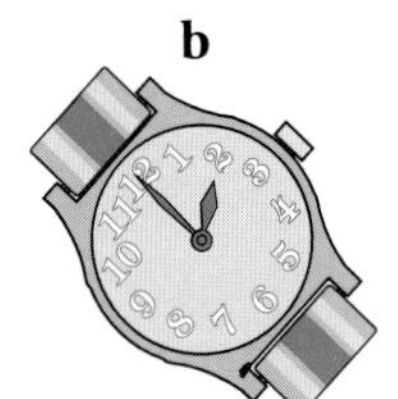

c

d

e

f

g

h

i

j

1 three fifteen
2 eight thirty
3 seven fifty-nine
4 two o'clock
5 four ten
6 nine forty
7 twelve o'clock
8 one thirty-two
9 six twenty
10 eleven thirty

2

QUIZ...

1 What time do people have dinner in Spain?
a 6.30
b 8.30
c 10.00

2 What time do shops close in France?
a 5.30
b 7.00
c 10.00

3 What time do banks open in Switzerland?
a 7.00
b 10.30
c 8.30

4 What time does school start in Korea?
a 7.30
b 9.00
c 8.00

5 What time do children finish school in Thailand?
a 3.30
b 4.00
c 4.30

3

Clock stretch

4

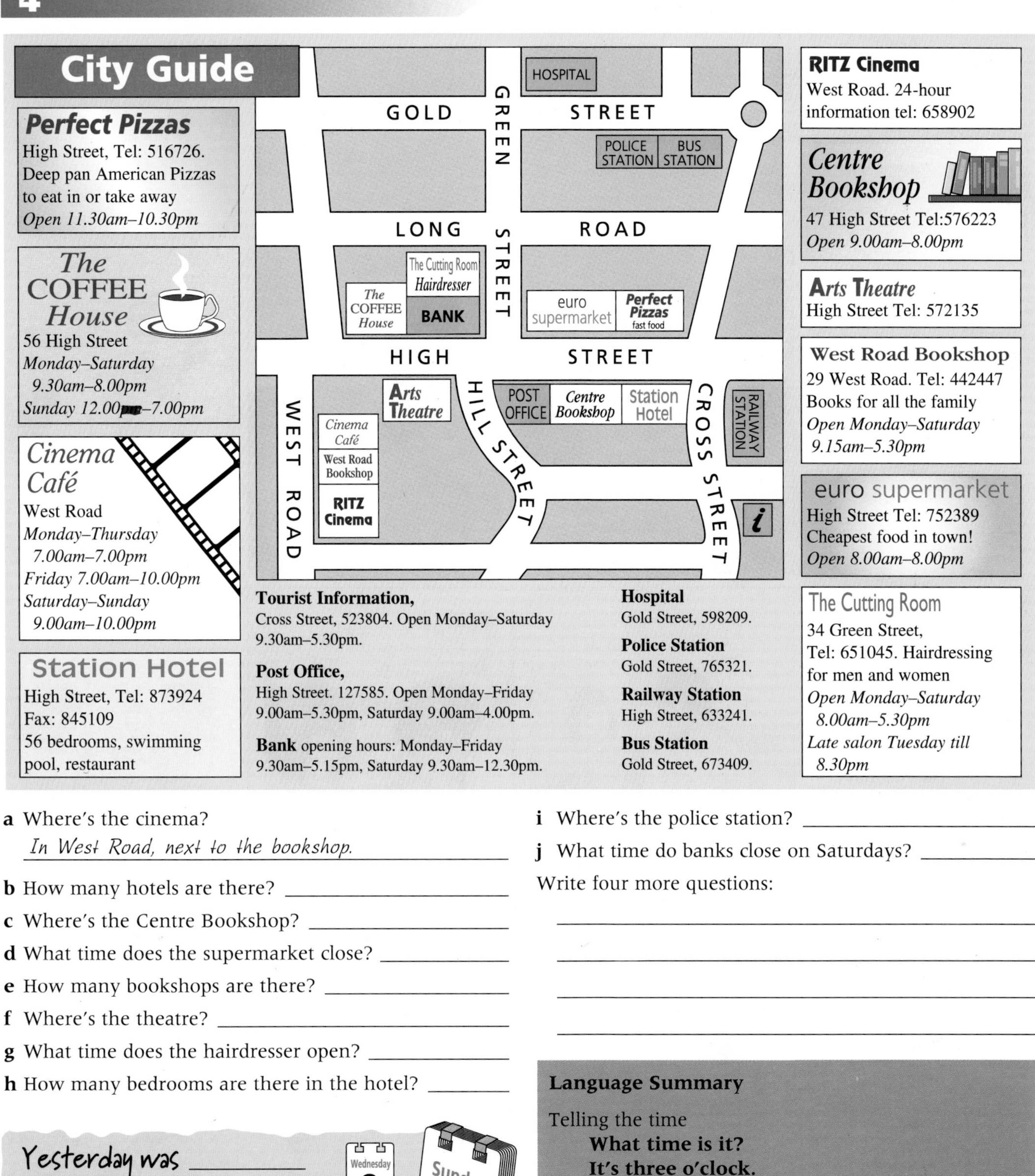

a Where's the cinema?
In West Road, next to the bookshop.

b How many hotels are there? ____________

c Where's the Centre Bookshop? ____________

d What time does the supermarket close? ____________

e How many bookshops are there? ____________

f Where's the theatre? ____________

g What time does the hairdresser open? ____________

h How many bedrooms are there in the hotel? ____________

i Where's the police station? ____________

j What time do banks close on Saturdays? ____________

Write four more questions:

____

____

____

____

Yesterday was ____________
Today is ____________
Tomorrow is ____________

Monday 1 · Friday 17 · Saturday 22 · Tuesday 8 · Wednesday 9 · Thursday 11 · Sunday 31

Language Summary

Telling the time
What time is it?
It's three o'clock.

Present simple questions
What time **does** the supermarket close?
What time **do** banks open?

see practice page 73

Lesson 2 *I'd like a room please*

Language focus: Buying a train ticket
Checking into a hotel
Filling in a form

1

1

1 When does the train leave?
2 Thank you.
3 That's £45.
4 At 10.30.
5 A single to Manchester, please. *a*
6 Here you are.

2

1 Yes. Single or double?
2 Yes, of course.
3 £40 per night.
4 Hello. Do you have a room?
5 I'd like a single room please. How much is it?
6 Can I see the room?

3

1 Good. How many nights do you want?
2 Thank you.
3 Two please.
4 Is that all right?
5 OK. Here's your key. Enjoy your stay.
6 Yes, fine.

2

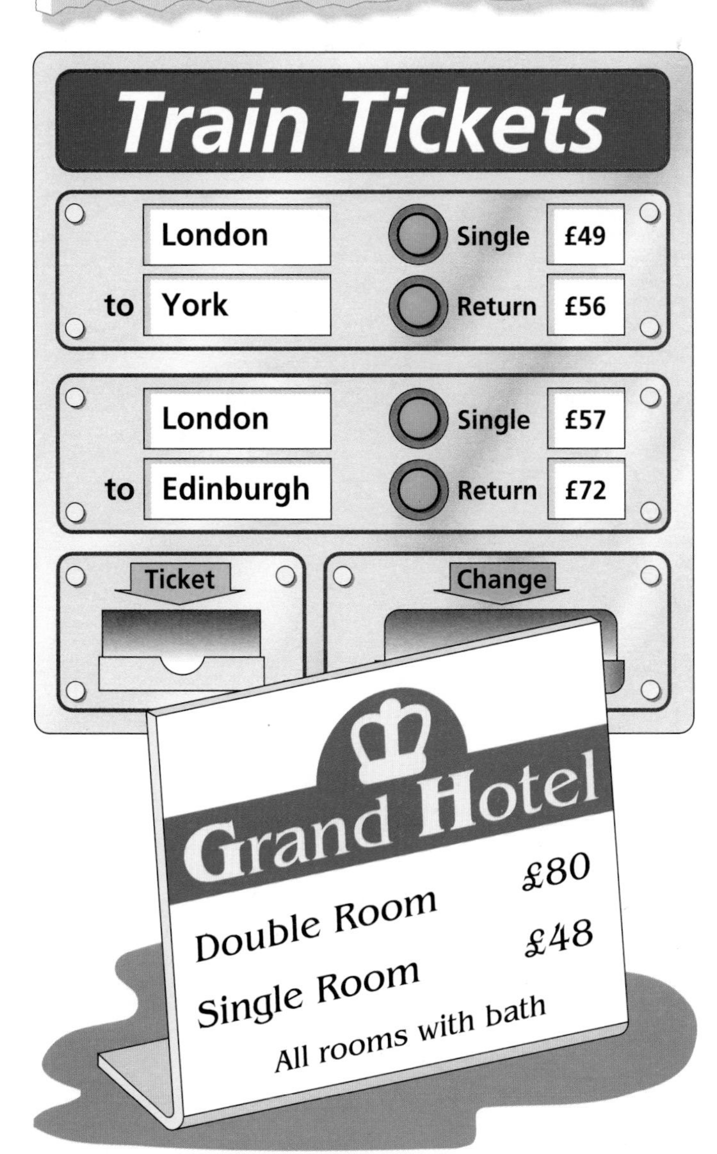

Train timetable				
London	07.30	09.10	12.30	15.10
York	09.25	10.59	14.32	17.15
Edinburgh	12.00	13.45	17.00	19.20

3

RENT A CAR
RENTACAR
Name:
Country:
Address: Capital Mansion 410,
3-5 Sakura-dori, Chuo-ku, Kobe.
Age:

How old are you?
Can I have your name, please?
What's your address?
Where are you from?

Name ....
Nationality ....
Address ....
....
Age ....

Language Summary

Buying a train ticket
A single to Manchester, please.

Checking into a hotel
I'd like a single room, please.

Filling in a form
What's your address?

see practice page 74

Lesson 3 *Winter sports*

Language focus: Review of units 1–3
have got

1

2

 **Bingo!**

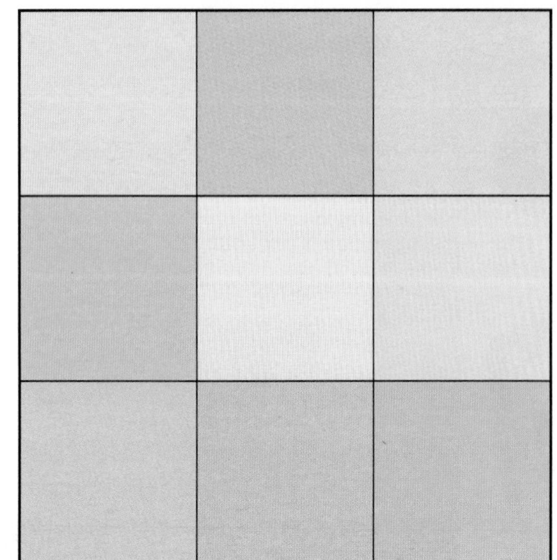

3

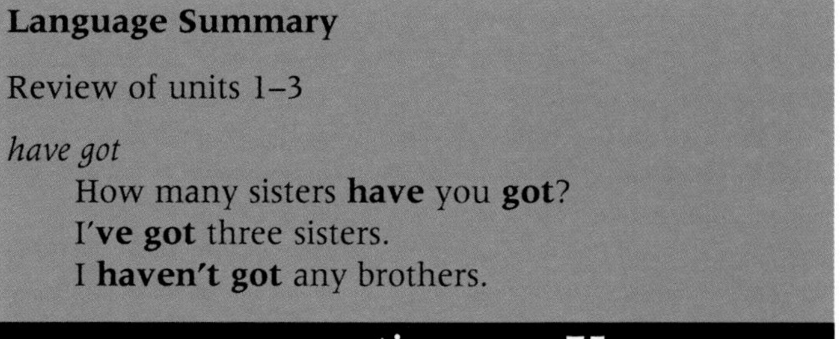

Language Summary

Review of units 1–3

have got

How many sisters **have** you **got**?
I'**ve got** three sisters.
I **haven't got** any brothers.

see practice page 75

Lesson 1 *What colour is it?*

Language focus: Colours

Vocabulary focus: Clothes

1

What colour is the skirt?
It's red.

What colour are the shoes?
They're black.

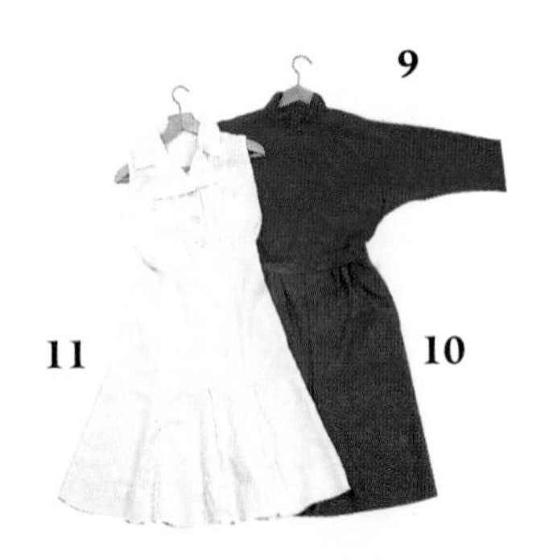
9
11
10

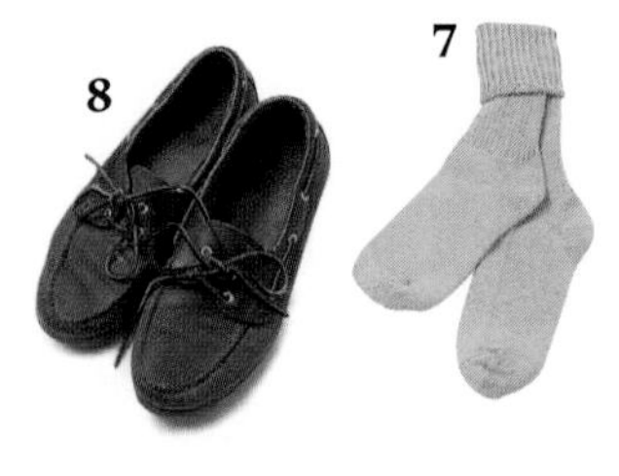
8
7

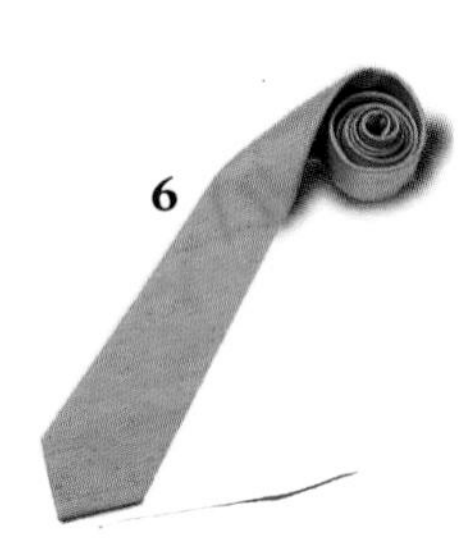
6

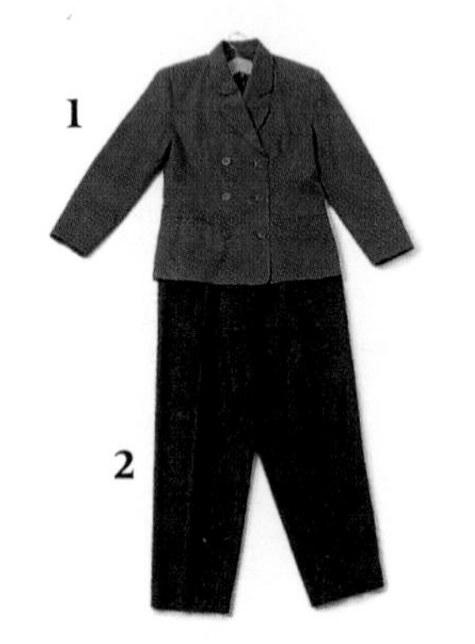
1
2

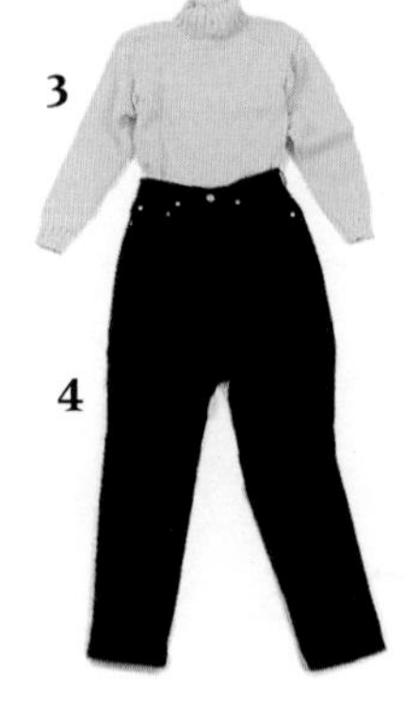
3
4

5

1 a *green* *jacket* **2** *dark* *blue* *trousers*

3 a ______ ______ **4** ______ ______

5 a ______ ______ **6** a ______ ______ ______

7 ______ ______ **8** ______ ______

9 a ______ ______ **10** a ______ ______

11 a ______ ______

2

 **Back to back**

3

4

My favourite shoes are green.

My favourite ________ ________ ________ .

My favourite ________ ________ ________ .

My favourite ________ ________ ________ .

My favourite ________ ________ ________ .

Language Summary

Colours

A **red** skirt.

What colour is the skirt? It's **red**.

see practice page 76

Lesson 2 *Can I try it on?*

Language focus: *can* for requests
too

1

2

C: = customer
SA: = shop assistant

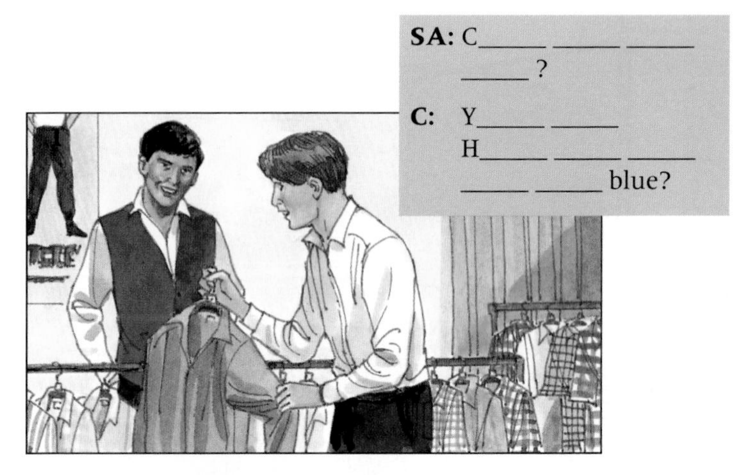

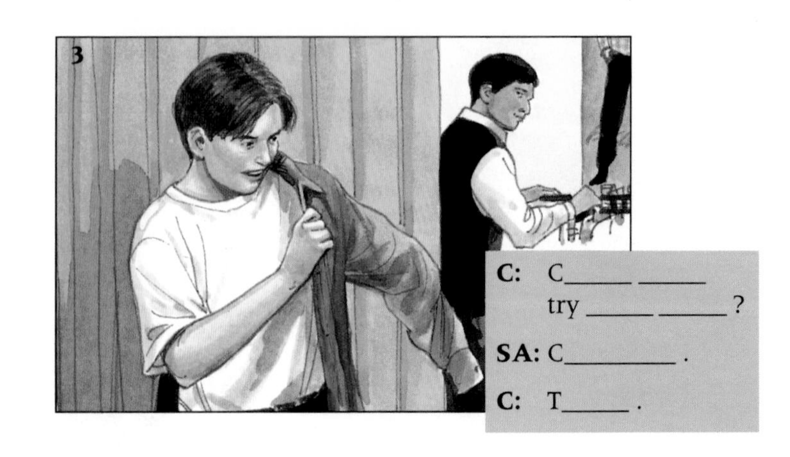

4

SA: I_____ _____ _____?

C: N_____, _____ too _____. H_____ _____ _____ _____ larger _____?

SA: Y_____. H_____ _____ _____.

5

SA: I_____ _____ _____?

C: Y_____, _____ _____.
I'_____ _____ _____.

Yesterday was _________
Today is _________
Tomorrow is _________
What's the date today? _________

Wednesday 9 · Sunday 31 · Thursday 11 · Saturday 22 · Friday 17 · Tuesday 8

3

What's different?

4

What size? ___

Have you got it in a larger size? ___

Can I help you? ___

Is it OK? _1_

Have you got this in blue? ___

Can I try it on? ___

5

Language Summary

can for requests

Can I try it on?

too

It's **too** small.

see practice page 77

Lesson 3 *How much is it?*

Language focus: *Let's*
going to

Vocabulary focus: Shops
Things to buy

1

2

Stretch!

3

How much is the watch?

50p *fifty p/pence*

£1.78 *one pound seventy-eight*

35p ______________________

90p ______________________

£2.99 ______________________

£9.89 ______________________

4

Yesterday was ________

Today is ________

Tomorrow is ________

What's the date today? ________

Wednesday 9 · Sunday 31 · Thursday 11 · Friday 17 · Saturday 22 · Tuesday 8

Language Summary

Let's …

Let's take a camera.

going to

We're going to take a camera.

see practice page 78

Lesson 1 *Do you like fish?*

Language focus: Present simple: *like, love, hate*
Vocabulary focus: Food: meals

1

1 2 3 4 5 6 7 8 9 10 11 12 13 14 15 16 17 18 19 20 21

☐ tea	☐ coffee	☐ milk
☐ water	1 fish	☐ prawns
☐ bread	☐ potatoes	☐ rice
☐ pasta	☐ chicken	☐ meat
☐ eggs	☐ cheese	☐ yoghurt
☐ carrots	☐ mushrooms	☐ tomatoes
☐ salad	☐ bananas	☐ oranges

2

Fruit and vegetables

3

What time do you have **breakfast?** ___________

What did you have for **breakfast?**

____

What time do you have **lunch?** ___________

What did you have for **lunch?**

____

What time do you have **dinner?** ___________

What did you have for **dinner?**

____

4

Do you like coffee?
Do you like bananas?

Yes, I love it/them.	*Yes, I do.*	*It's/They're OK.*	*No, I don't.*	*No, I hate it/them.*

____

____

____

____

____

____

Language Summary

Present simple: *like, love, hate*

Do you like rice/oranges?
Yes, **I love** it/them.
Yes, **I do**.
It's/They're OK.
No, **I don't**.
No, **I hate** it/them.

see practice page 79

Lesson 2 *Have you got any prawns?*

Language focus: Present simple: *have got, need*
Countable and uncountable nouns
any

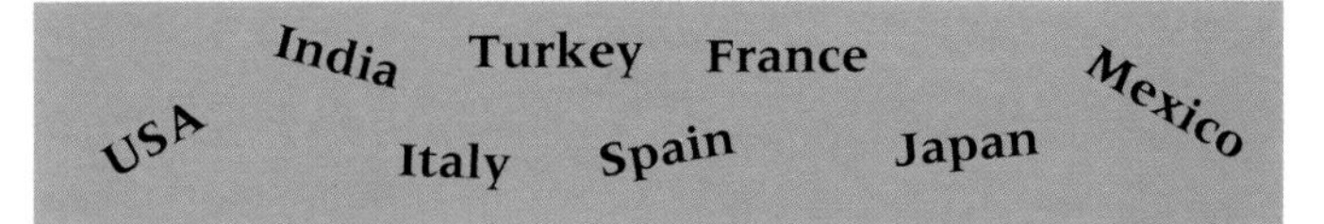

USA
India
Italy
Turkey
Spain
France
Japan
Mexico

1

Mushroom pizza

Quiche

Sukiyaki

Chicken curry

Mole

Paëlla

Cheeseburger

Lamb Kebab

2

1 ______

flour
eggs
bacon
cheese

2 ______

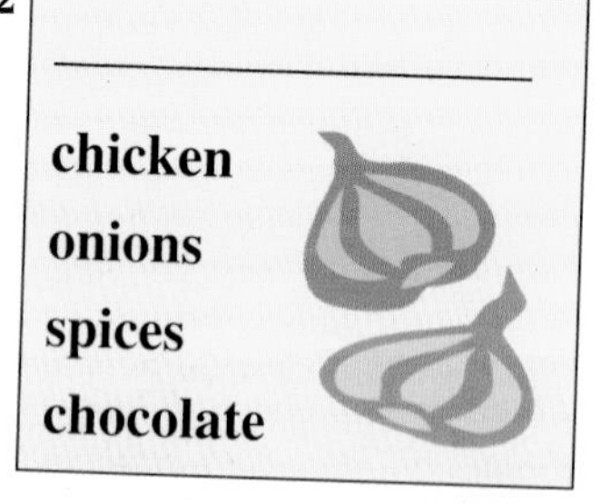
chicken
onions
spices
chocolate

3 ______

lamb
bread
onions
tomato

4 ______

beef
mushrooms
soy sauce
rice

5 ______

flour
tomatoes
cheese
mushrooms

6 ______

chicken
spices
onions
rice

7 ______

bread
beef
onions
cheese

8 ______

rice
prawns
onions
chicken

3

It and them

4

True or false?

a Fabio and Marta are making chicken curry. _T_

b Fabio and Marta have got spices and onions. _____

c The Americans are making pizza. _____

d The Americans have got spices and onions. _____

e The Americans need spices. _____

f The Americans need onions. _____

5

Yesterday was _____
Today is _____
Tomorrow is _____
What's the date today? _____
Wednesday 9
Sunday 31
Thursday 11
Friday 17
Saturday 22
Tuesday 8

6

Language Summary

Present simple: *have got, need*

Have you **got** any bread?
Yes, but **I need** it.

Countable and uncountable nouns

Have you got any **mushrooms**?
Yes, but I need **them**.
Have you got any **cheese**?
Yes, but I need **it**.

any

Have you got **any** cheese?

see practice page 80

Lesson 3 *What would you like?*

Language focus: *would like*
I'll have

1

tacos

spring rolls

omelette

ice cream

french fries

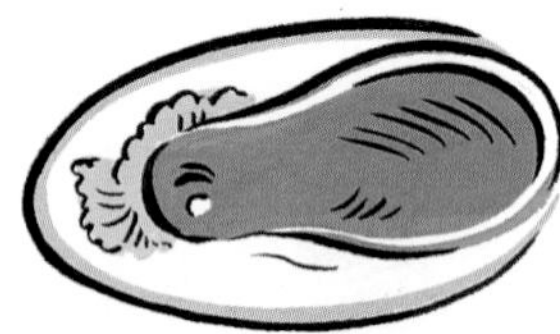
steak

milk shake

chocolate cake

beer

Café

Starters

____

____

____

Main Courses

____

____

____

____

____

____

Desserts

____

____

____

Drinks

____

____

____

____

____

____

2

1

- [ ] Would you like anything to drink?
- [ ] A table for two, please.
- [ ] Yes, I'll have paëlla and salad, please.
- [ ] OK.
- [ ] Are you ready to order?
- [1] Hello.
- [ ] Certainly.
- [ ] Yes, a beer and a cola, please.
- [ ] I'd like spring rolls and then steak, french fries and mushrooms, please.

2

- [ ] Can I have the bill, please?
- [ ] Yes, please. I'll have ice cream and coffee.
- [ ] Certainly.
- [ ] Anything else?
- [ ] Thank you. Bye.
- [ ] Just coffee for me, please.
- [ ] Bye.

1

Waiter: ______________
Customer 1: ______________
Waiter: ______________

Waiter: ______________
Customer 1: ______________
____
Customer 2: ______________
____
Waiter: ______________
Customer 1: ______________
____
Waiter: ______________

2

Waiter: ______________
Customer 1: ______________
Customer 2: ______________

Customer 1: ______________
Waiter: ______________

Waiter: ______________
Customer 1, 2: ______________

Yesterday was ______________
Today is ______________
Tomorrow is ______________
What's the date today? ______________

Thursday 11 · Wednesday 9 · Sunday 31 · Friday 17 · Saturday 22 · Tuesday 8

Language Summary

would like

I'd like a pizza, please.
Would you like any coffee?

I'll have

I'll have ice cream, please.

see practice page 81

Lesson 1 *She's taller than me*

Language focus: Comparison of adjectives
Vocabulary focus: Parts of the body

1

- ☐ elbow
- ☑ 1 head
- ☐ finger
- ☐ eye
- ☐ chest
- ☐ cheek
- ☐ knee
- ☐ tongue
- ☐ ear
- ☐ nose
- ☐ shoulder

- ☐ arm
- ☐ eyebrow
- ☐ hand
- ☐ hair
- ☐ thumb
- ☐ chin
- ☐ stomach
- ☐ neck
- ☐ leg
- ☐ mouth
- ☐ foot

2

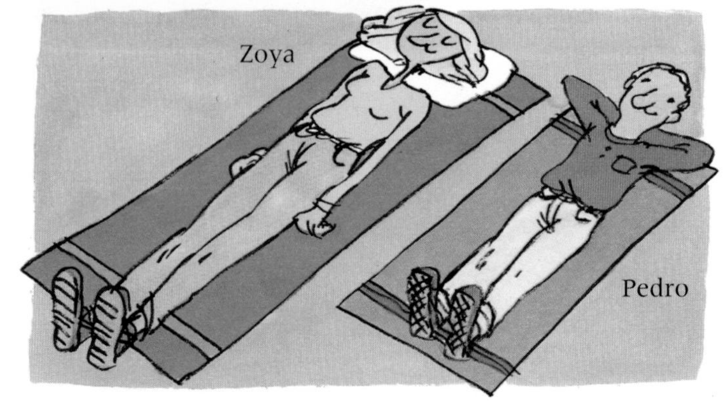

Zoya is taller than Pedro.

Zoya's hair is longer ______ Pedro's.

Zoya's hair is ______ ______ ______ .

Zoya's feet ______ ______ ______ ______ .

3

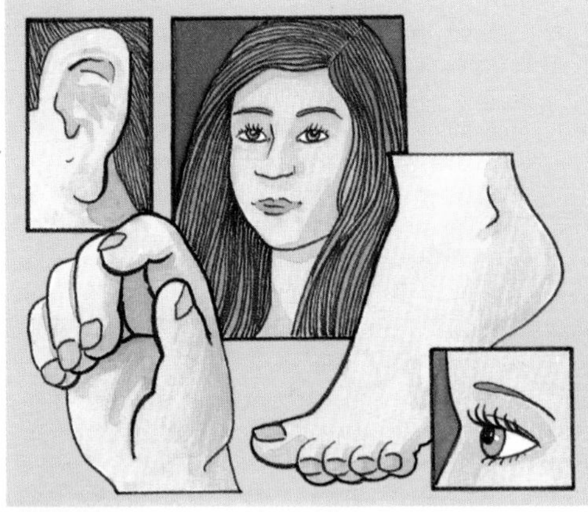

1 'I am ______ than ______.'

2 'My ______ is ______ than ______'s.'

3 'My ______.'

4 'My ______.'

5 'My ______.'

4

1 ______ 2 ______ 3 ______ 4 ______ 5 ______

What are their names?

a Erol is taller than Frank.

b Adam's hair is lighter than Jordi's.

c Frank's ears are bigger than Jordi's.

d Pascal is shorter than Frank.

e Erol's hair is darker than Jordi's.

f Adam's ears are smaller than Pascal's.

g Jordi's hair is shorter than Pascal's.

h Erol's hair is longer than Pascal's.

i Jordi is taller than Adam.

j Pascal's hair is darker than Frank's.

k Frank's hair is shorter than Adam's.

l Erol's ears are smaller than Frank's.

Language Summary

Comparison of adjectives

Zoya is **taller than** Pedro.

Pedro's hair is **shorter than** Zoya's.

see practice page 82

Lesson 2 *What's the matter?*

Language focus: Present simple negative
should

Vocabulary focus: Ailments

1

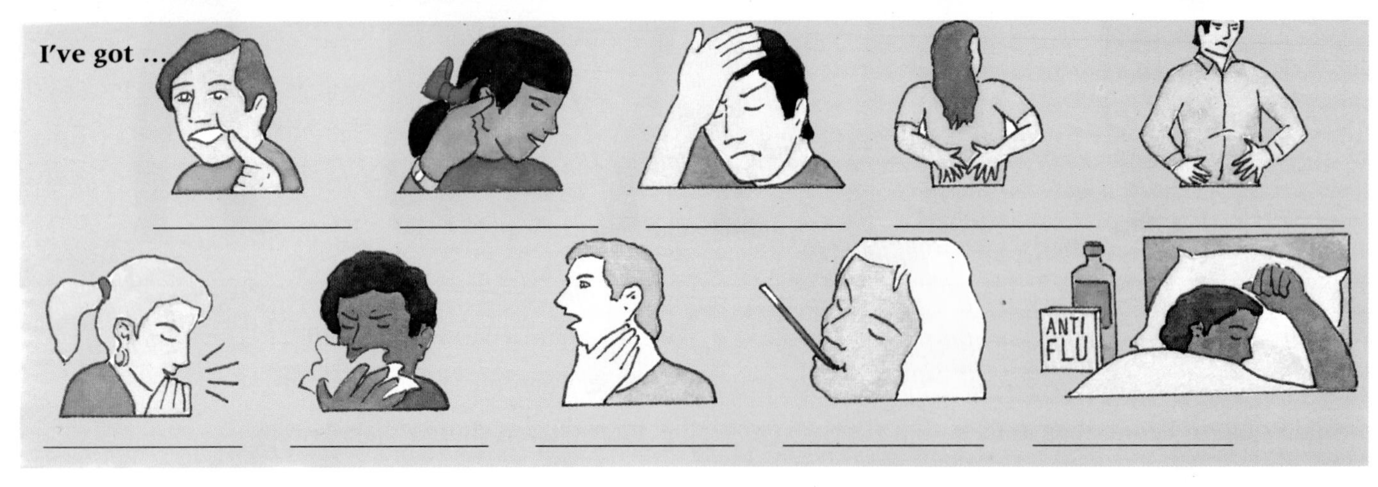

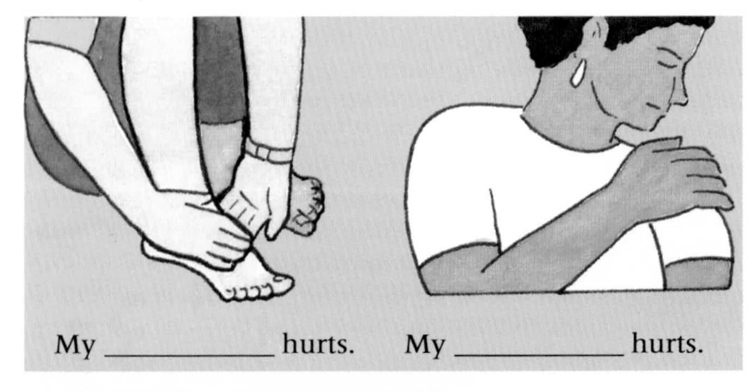

2

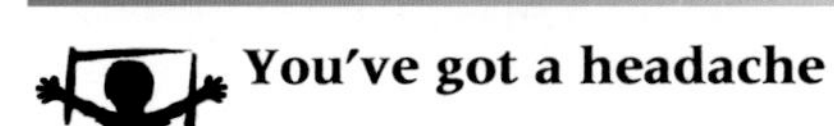

3

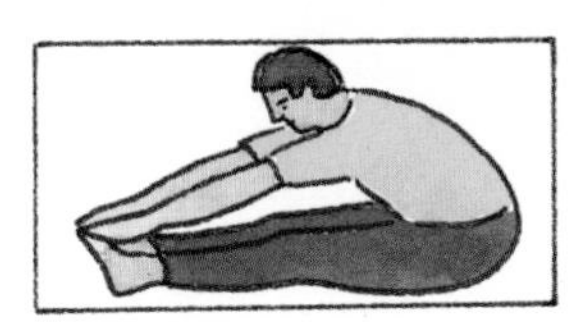

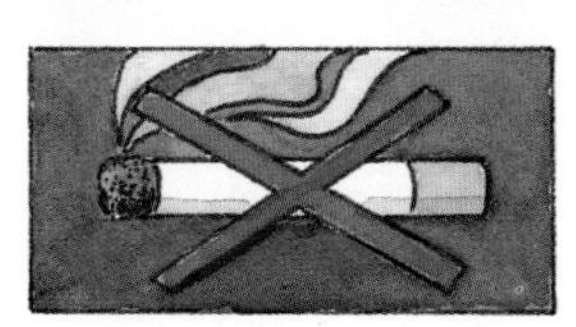

You should ...

take an aspirin

go to bed

stop smoking

keep warm

eat nothing

take some exercise

drink a lot of water

go to the doctor

4

____________________ ____________________

____

Language Summary

Present simple negative

I don't feel very well.

She doesn't feel very well.

should

I think you **should** take an asprin.

see practice page 83

Lesson 3 *What a wonderful world*

Language focus: Review of units 4–6

1

World quiz

1 Which is longer? The River Amazon or the River Nile?
2 Which is larger? Chile or Turkey?
3 Which is bigger? A lion or a tiger?
4 Which is wetter? London or Chicago?
5 Which is older? The Pyramids or The Great Wall of China?
6 Which is hotter? Delhi or Singapore?
7 Which is colder? The Arctic or the Antarctic?
8 Which is taller? The Eiffel Tower or the Empire State Building?

2

Do it!

3

Do you like red?

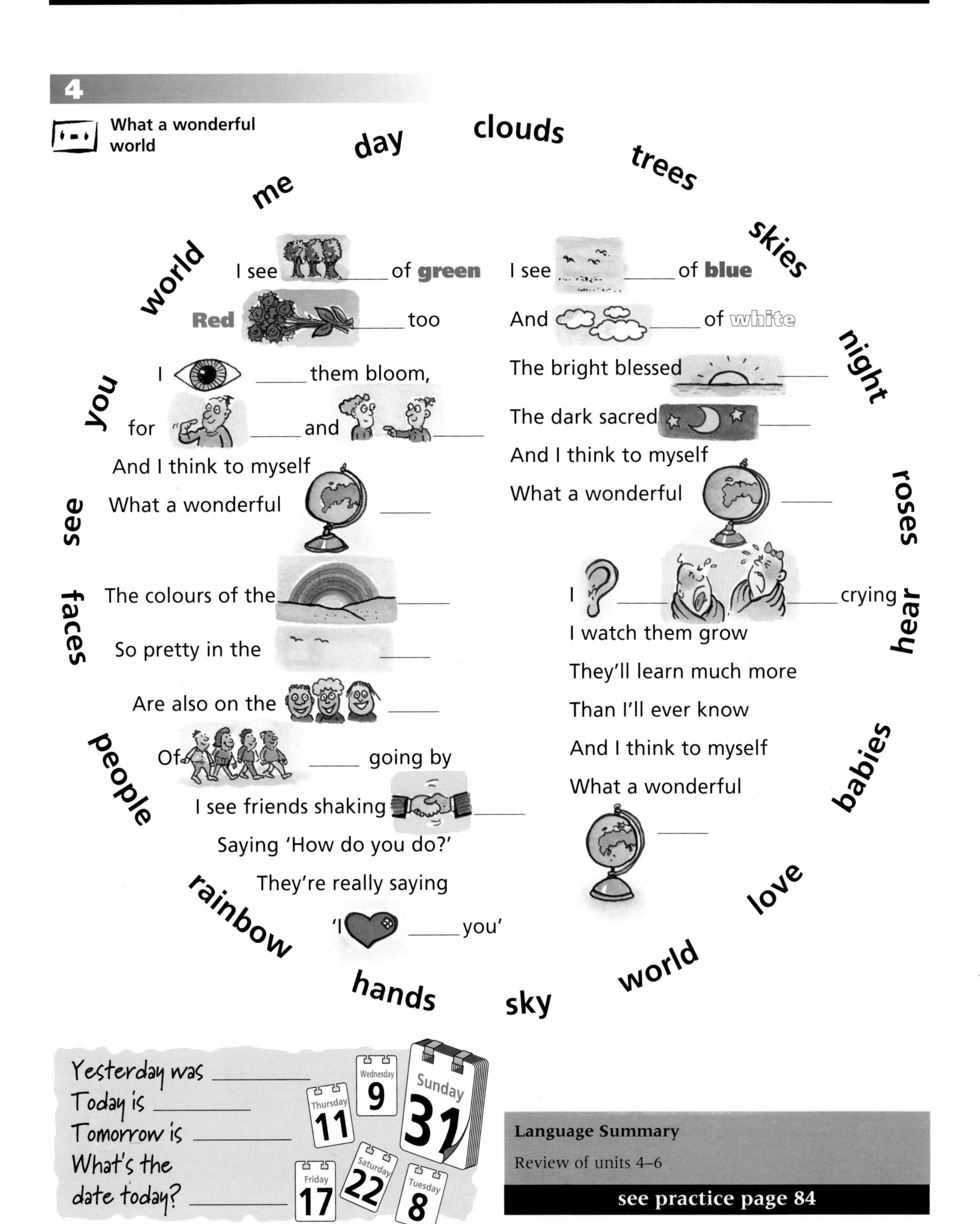
4
What a wonderful world
day
clouds
trees
me
skies
world
night
you
roses
see
hear
faces
babies
people
love
rainbow
world
hands
sky
I see ____ of green
Red ____ too
I ____ them bloom,
for ____ and ____
And I think to myself
What a wonderful ____
I see ____ of blue
And ____ of white
The bright blessed ____
The dark sacred ____
And I think to myself
What a wonderful ____
The colours of the ____
So pretty in the ____
Are also on the ____
Of ____ going by
I see friends shaking ____
Saying 'How do you do?'
They're really saying
'I ____ you'
I ____ ____ crying
I watch them grow
They'll learn much more
Than I'll ever know
And I think to myself
What a wonderful ____
Yesterday was ____
Today is ____
Tomorrow is ____
What's the date today? ____
Wednesday 9
Sunday 31
Thursday 11
Saturday 22
Friday 17
Tuesday 8
Language Summary
Review of units 4–6
see practice page 84

Lesson 1 *When do you get up?*

Language focus: Present simple for daily routines
so do I
Telling the time: *past, to*

1

1 *I wake up* ______.

2 ______.

3 ______.

4 ______.

5 ______.

6 ______.

7 ______.

8 ______.

2

1 *half past six*

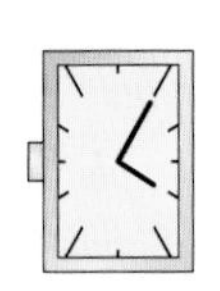

2 ______

3 ______

4 ______

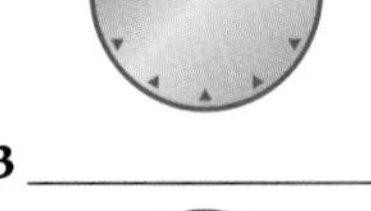

5 ______

6 ______

7 ______

8 ______

9 ______

10 ______

11 ______

3

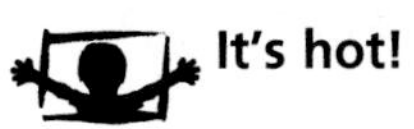

It's hot!

4

Pluto's Day

I wake up at seven o'clock and watch television – I love cartoons.

wake up

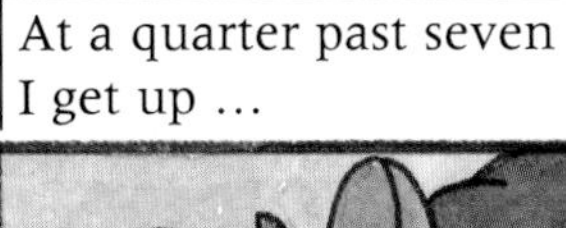

get up

do exercises

have breakfast

have a shower

go for a walk

have lunch

go home

5

What time do you have lunch?
What do you do in the evening?

	Me	My partner
get up		
have breakfast		
go to work/school		
have lunch		
finish work/school		
________		
________		
________		
go to bed		

Language Summary

Present simple for daily routines

I wake up at seven o'clock.
She wakes up at seven o'clock.

so do I

Fernanda goes to work at half past seven and **so do I**.

Telling the time: *past, to*

8.30 = **half past** eight.
8.45 = **a quarter to** nine.

see practice page 85

Lesson 2 *Do you like swimming?*

Language focus: *like -ing*
Vocabulary focus: Sports and hobbies

1

Match

______ dancing ☐
______ playing football ☐
______ cooking ☐
______ flying ☐
______ watching TV ☐
______ sleeping ☐
______ swimming ☐
______ playing volleyball ☐
______ listening to music ☐
______ shopping ☐
______ travelling ☐
______ reading ☐
______ going to the gym ☐
______ running ☐
______ going to the cinema ☐

2

I think you really like watching TV.

I really like

I like

I quite like

I don't like

3

What do you like doing in your free time?

I really like ______________________________.

I like ______________________________.

I quite like ______________________________.

4

 **If ...**

5

I really like flying, but I don't like kryptonite. Who am I?

You're Superman!

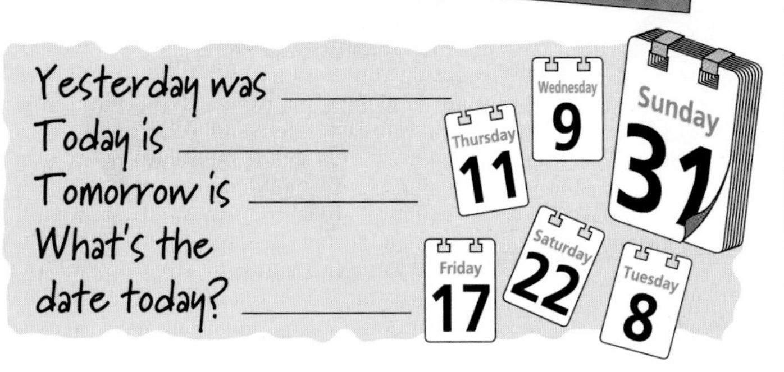

6

In English classes, do you like ...	Me	My group
speaking English?		
listening?		
reading?		
writing?		
learning grammar?		
learning words?		
playing games?		
working alone?		
working with other learners?		
miming?		
doing homework?		
using this book?		

Language Summary

like -ing

Do you **like** swim**ming**?
I quite like it.
She really likes it.

see practice page 86

Lesson 3 *Can you ride a motorbike?*

Language focus: *can* for ability
Adverbs of manner

1

Cán you play the gui[tar]? Yes, I [can].

No, I can't.

I cán ________ but I can't ________.

play the guitar

play chess

sing

Bonjour

speak French

water-ski

draw

use a computer

2

Jobs • Jobs • Jobs

Write for our travel magazine

Work as an assistant for a film company

Sail Around the World!

DRIVE A TRUCK ACROSS
SOUTH AMERICA

Work in a
summer
camp
for kids!

Join a travelling theatre company!

Yesterday was ________
Today is ________
Tomorrow is ________
What's the date today? ________

Wednesday 9 Thursday 11 Sunday 31 Saturday 22 Friday 17 Tuesday 8

3

He's a good player. He plays **1** _well_______.

I'm a bad cook. I cook **2** __________.

She's a beautiful dancer. She dances **3** __________.

You're a dangerous driver. You drive **4** __________.

We're safe drivers. We drive **5** __________.

He's very quiet. He talks **6** __________.

Children like noisy games. They play games **7** __________.

He's a slow runner. He runs **8** __________.

She's a fast swimmer. She swims **9** __________.

4

True or false?

a He's driving dangerously. _T_

b She's singing well. ___

c He's speaking slowly. ___

d He's playing the drums quietly. ___

e He's walking fast. ___

5

Hello!
Loudly

Language Summary

can for ability
I **can** swim but I **can't** water-ski.

Adverbs of manner
He can play the guitar **well** but he sings **badly**.

see practice page 87

Lesson 1 *What was your holiday like?*

Language focus: Past simple: *was, were*
Past simple
Vocabulary focus: Holidays, weather

1

1 Where did she go?

a  b  c 

2 What _____ the weather like?

d  e  f 

3 What _____ her room like?

g  h  i 

4 What _____ the food like?

j  k  l 

5 What _____ the people like?

m  n  o 

2

What was your holiday like? *It* *was* _______ .

What was the weather like? It _____ _______ .

What was the food like? ___ _____ _______ .

What was your room like? ___ _____ _______ .

What was the place like? ___ _____ _______ .

3

Dear Maria,

I'm sorry I didn't write to you before, but I was too busy having a wonderful time.

I met a very good-looking man on the first evening and we danced all night.

We swam and sunbathed every day and ate and drank a lot in the evenings. I bought some beautiful clothes. I didn't have time to read any books.

Love,

Clara

Maria Simms
452 Ash Road
Bath BA3 6BS
England

Present/Infinitive	Past
go	*went*
buy	_______
dance	_______
drink	_______
eat	_______
meet	_______
sunbathe	_______

4

Follow your teacher!

5

Student A

Last week ________ ______ ________ went camping _____ ______ _____________ . It was cold but __________ ______ ______ ______ were very beautiful. ________ ______ ______ _________ and climbed a mountain _______ _______ .

Where did they go?

a

b

c

6

Yesterday was ____________
Today is ____________
Tomorrow is ____________
What's the date today? ____________

Wednesday 9 · Sunday 31 · Thursday 11 · Friday 17 · Saturday 22 · Tuesday 8

Language Summary

Past simple: *was/were*
What **was** the weather like?
What **were** the people like?
Past simple
Where **did** they **go**?
They **went** to the mountains.
They **didn't go** to the beach.

see practice page 88

Lesson 2 *The singing burglar*

Language focus: Past simple: regular and irregular verbs
Joining sentences

1

burglar

Mr and Mrs Angelos

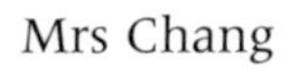

Mrs Chang

2

What happened next?

3

Draw the word

4

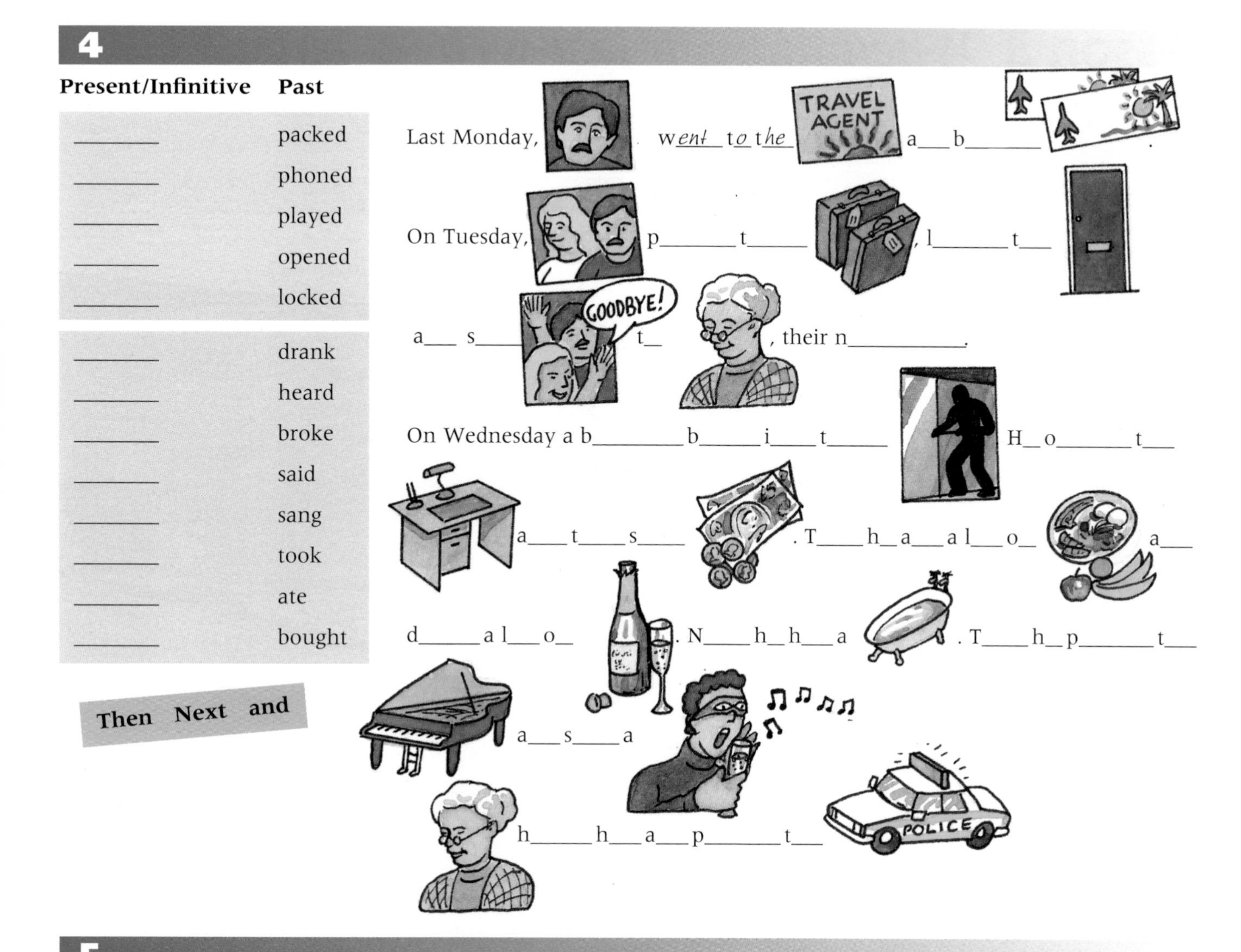

Present/Infinitive	Past
______	packed
______	phoned
______	played
______	opened
______	locked
______	drank
______	heard
______	broke
______	said
______	sang
______	took
______	ate
______	bought

Then Next and

Last Monday, ______ w*ent* t*o* t*he* ______ a__ b______ ______.

On Tuesday, ______ p______ t______ ______, l______ t__ ______

a__ s______ ______ t__ ______, their n__________.

On Wednesday a b________ b______ i____ t______ ______ H__ o______ t__

______ a___ t____ s____ ______. T____ h__ a___ a l___ o__ ______ a___

d______ a l___ o__ ______. N____ h__ h___ a ______. T____ h__ p______ t___

______ a___ s____ a ______

______ h______ h___ a___ p______ t___ ______

5

Buy

Buy

Yesterday was ____________

Today is ____________

Tomorrow is ____________

What's the date today? ____________

Thursday 11 · Wednesday 9 · Sunday 31 · Friday 17 · Saturday 22 · Tuesday 8

Language Summary

Past simple: regular and irregular verbs

Mrs Chang **phoned** the police.

He **bought** two tickets to Hawaii.

Joining sentences

He played the piano **and** sang a song. **Then** he had a bath.

see practice page 89

Lesson 3 *When did you last write a letter?*

Language focus: Times in the past
Vocabulary focus: Months of the year

1

Months

1 aaryjnu ________
2 ujen ________
3 sutgua ________
4 oortbec ________
5 ayrrfbeu ________

2

When was ...?

yesterday ________

last	night	________
	week	________
	month	________
	year	________

the day before yesterday ________

the	night	before last	________
	week		________
	month		________
	year		________

three	days	ago	________
	nights		________
	weeks		________
	months		________
	years		________

3

When did you last ...	Name	When
go to the cinema?		
play a sport?		
write a letter or fax?		
take a photo?		
go to the dentist?		
have a haircut?		
phone someone?		
eat some rice?		
go to a disco?		
go on holiday?		
buy new clothes?		
talk to an animal?		
kiss someone?		

4

Where did you go?

How did you get there?

Who were you with?

What did you eat?

When did you go there?

What did you do?

Yesterday was ________
Today is ________
Tomorrow is ________
What's the date today? ________

Wednesday 9 · Thursday 11 · Sunday 31 · Friday 17 · Saturday 22 · Tuesday 8

Language Summary

Times in the past
I saw him **last night**.
When did you last have a haircut?
Three weeks ago.

see practice page 90

Lesson 1 *What's he doing?*

Language focus: Present continuous

1

1 I'__	sightsee____.
2 She'__	water-ski____.
3 It'__	rain____.
4 We'__	play____ cards.

5 They'__	shop____.
6 I'__	____ work____.
7 We'__	____ ski____.
8 ____ you	have____ a good time?

2

You're wearing his watch!

3

Love ____________

4

Language Summary

Present continuous

I'm reading.

see practice page 91

Lesson 2 *What's on?*

Language focus: Making suggestions
Saying what you want

Vocabulary focus: Entertainments

1

Films

- ☐ comedy
- ☐ thriller
- ☐ horror
- ☐ cartoon
- ☐ adventure

Theatre

- ☐ musical
- ☐ play

☐ **Disco/Night Club**

☐ **Ballet**

Concert

- ☐ classical
- ☐ jazz
- ☐ pop/rock

Restaurants

- ☐ fast food
- ☐ Chinese
- ☐ Indian
- ☐ French
- ☐ Italian

2

a No, I don't like ________ films. I'd rather see ________ .
b We always eat ________ .
c I'd rather go to the ________ .
d What shall we do tonight?
e OK. Let's go out for a meal.
f What's on?

g Why don't we go to the ________ ?
h No, not that.
i ________ and ________ . What about ________ ?
j All right. What about the ________ ? It's very good.
k Oh, OK then.

Yesterday was ________
Today is ________
Tomorrow is ________
What's the date today? ________

Thursday 11 · Wednesday 9 · Sunday 31 · Friday 17 · Saturday 22 · Tuesday 8

3

Sit down if ...

4

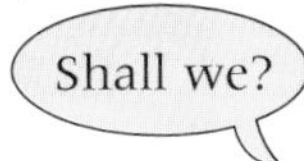

Shall we go to the cinema?

Teacher: Let's go to the cinema.
Student: Let's go to the cinema.
Teacher: the Chinese restaurant.
Student: Let's go to the Chinese restaurant.
Teacher: Shall we?
Student: Shall we go to the Chinese restaurant?
Teacher: the theatre
Student: Shall we go to the theatre?

5

Let's go to the jazz concert.

No, I hate jazz!

Language Summary

Making suggestions
Shall we go to the theatre?
Let's go to the cinema.
Saying what you want
I'd rather go to the disco.

see practice page 92

Lesson 3 *Are you free tonight?*

Language focus: Prepositions of time
Present continuous for the future
Making suggestions

1

2

What's Tom doing …

1 at 8.30 pm on Monday? He's ________________.

2 at 3.30 pm on Tuesday? He's ________________.

3 at 10.00 am on Wednesday? He's ________________.

4 at 2.00 pm on Thursday? He's ________________.

5 at 12.00 pm on Friday? He's ________________.

6 at 2.30 pm on Friday? He's ________________.

3

Jazz Chant

A: Can you see me this morning at quarter to ten?

B: No, I'm having a meeting then.

A: What about later? A quarter past three?

B: No, my grandmother's coming to tea.

4

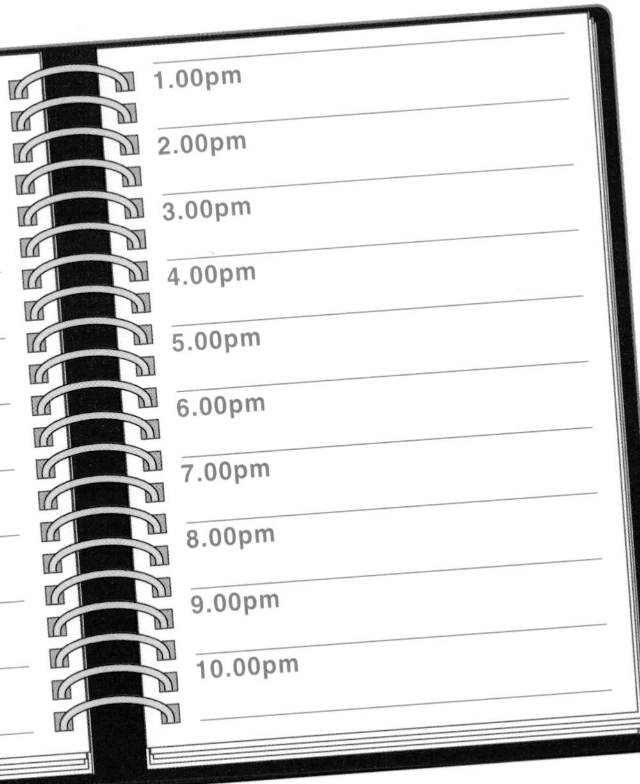

1.00pm
2.00pm
3.00pm
4.00pm
5.00pm
6.00pm
7.00pm
8.00pm
9.00pm
10.00pm

Language Summary

Prepositions of time
- **at** four o'clock
- **in** the morning
- **on** Monday

Present continuous for the future
- **I'm seeing** my mother at 8.30 tonight.

Making suggestions
- **Would you like to** have dinner with me?
- **What about** Thursday?

see practice page 93

Lesson 1 *The news*

Language focus: Revision of past simple
Present continuous for the future

Vocabulary focus: Revision: weather, sports, numbers

1

1

2

3

4

5

2

True or false?

1 A plane crashed in Canada this morning. T
2 Fourteen people died. ____
3 Joe Wild married Suzy Presley last week. ____
4 Joe and Suzy are having their honeymoon in Bali. ____
5 The Prime Minister went to France yesterday. ____
6 He is staying in Paris for two days. ____
7 A German woman gave birth to six boys last night. ____
8 Mrs Schneider's six children are ill. ____
9 There was a football match between Italy and Brazil last night. ____
10 The football match is in Italy.____

3

T____ P______ M________ i___ a________ i___ P______
t____ a________ t____ v____ t___ F______ P________.

4

Stretch!

5

What did Merve ask Joe?

1 When did you first meet Suzy? ☐
2 How many people were at the wedding? ☐
3 How much did it cost? ☐
4 What's the weather like? ☐
5 How was the wedding? ☐
6 What did you see? ☐
7 When did it happen? ☐
8 How long are you staying in Bali? ☐
9 What happened? ☐
10 How do you feel? ☐

Joe said:

Two weeks ago.
Five hundred.
Fantastic!
A week.

6

Yesterday was ________
Today is ________
Tomorrow is ________
What's the date today? ________

Wednesday 9
Sunday 31
Thursday 11
Friday 17
Saturday 22
Tuesday 8

Language Summary

Revision of past simple
Joe Wild **married** Suzy Presley yesterday.

Present continuous for the future
Tonight Italy **are playing** Brazil.

see practice page 94

Lesson 2 *Homeward bound*

Language focus: Revision

1

What's Paul's job?

Railway Hotel

Dear Cathy
It's three o'clock in the morning and I can't sleep because I'm thinking of you. I arrived here this afternoon by train. This town is like all the others – grey apartment blocks and dirty streets. But the concert was good – everybody liked my music. I'm very tired and I want to come home – only three more towns to visit!

I love you.
Paul xx

Answer these questions:

1 Who is Cathy?

2 How does Paul feel?

3 What does he want to do?

2

3

 *Homeward Bound* by Paul Simon.

__ My suitcase and guitar in hand
__ Got a ticket for my destination
_1_ I'm sitting in the railway station
__ For a poet and a one-man band
__ On a tour of one night stands
__ And every stop is neatly planned

Homeward bound, I wish I was
Homeward bound
Home, where my thoughts escaping
Home, where my music's playing
Home, where my love lies waiting silently for me

__ And every stranger's face I see
__ And each town looks the same to me
__ Reminds me that I long to be
__ Of cigarettes and magazines
__ The movies and the factories
__ Every day is an endless stream

Homeward bound, I wish I was
Homeward bound
Home, where my thoughts escaping
Home, where my music's playing
Home, where my love lies waiting silently for me

4

Mime the word

5

Where did you go?

	Teacher	Me	My partner
Where?			
When?			
How?			
Who with?			
Feelings?			

Language Summary

Revision

see practice page 95

Lesson 3 *Travel Game*

Collect a passport, visa, plane ticket and traveller's cheques, and then fly to Sydney, New York, Dublin or Singapore!

How to play

- Use a dice and counters.
- Start at the airport.
- Choose the direction to go in.
- You can change the direction when you go to an airport, or a square like this:
- Answer questions when you land on a question square.
- If you answer correctly, have another turn.
- Collect passport, ticket, traveller's cheques and a visa.
- Tick ✔ the picture in the table.

- To get into a city you must have the right visa.
- If you can't answer the question, look for it in your book.
- **You can only look in your book three times in the game!** When you look in your book tick one of the *book* boxes.

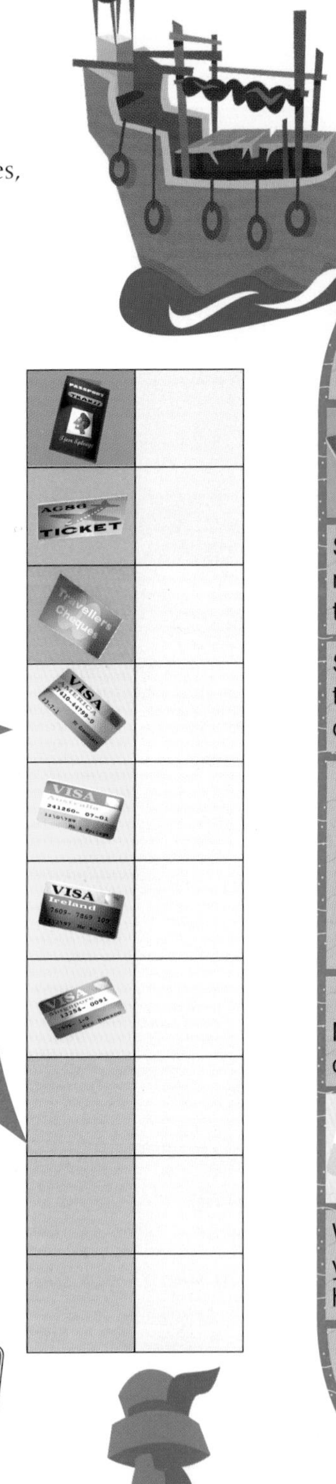

Special squares

One of the group asks you a question beginning with the word on the square.

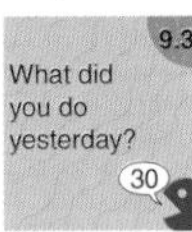

9.3
What did you do yesterday?
30

Answer the question. Talk for 30 seconds!

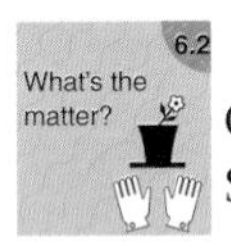

6.2
What's the matter?

One of the group mimes. Say what's the matter with them.

Yesterday was ______
Today is ______
Tomorrow is ______
What's the date today? ______
Wednesday 9
Thursday 11
Sunday 31
Friday 17
Saturday 22
Tuesday 8

Language Summary

Revision

see practice page 96

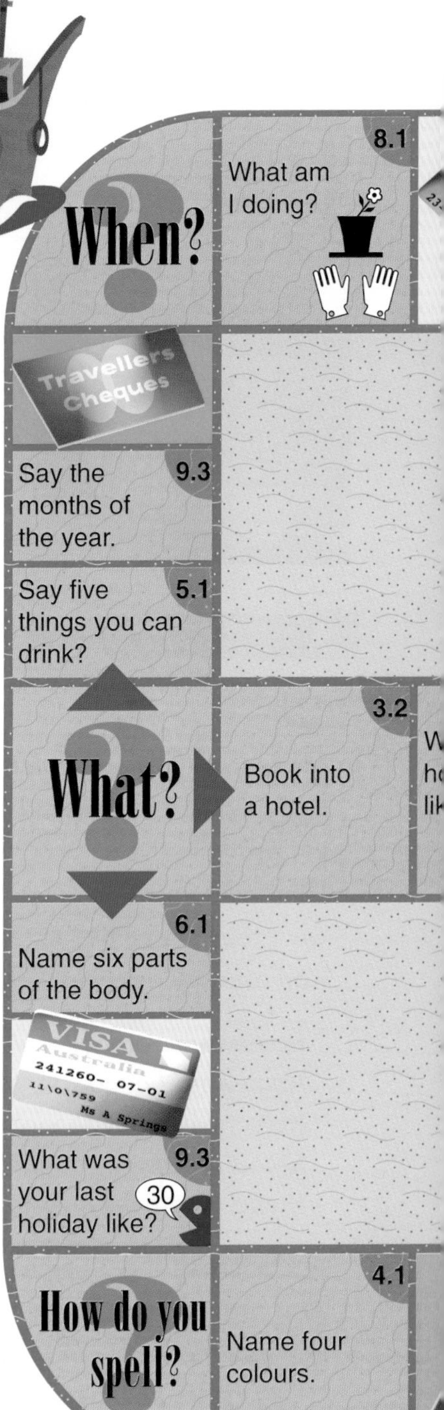

Singapore
When?
What am I doing?
8.1
Travellers Cheques
Say the months of the year.
9.3
Say five things you can drink?
5.1
What?
Book into a hotel.
3.2
Name six parts of the body.
6.1
VISA Australia 241260- 07-01 11\0\759 Ms A Springs
What was your last holiday like?
9.3
30
How do you spell?
Name four colours.
4.1
New York

Dublin
5.1
What did you have for breakfast? lunch? dinner?
Where?
7.3
Say three things you can do and three things you can't do.
PASSPORT
TKAKJJ
9.3
What did you do yesterday?
30
How do you spell?
What's your bedroom like?
2.3
30
3.1
Say the days of the week.
AG86
TICKET
Say five things you like doing in your free time.
7.2
Name and spell three countries.
1.1
What colour is the fourth colour of the rainbow?
4.1
2.1
PASSPORT
FUJ X 17033
AIRPORT
1.2
Say four jobs.
2.2
How do you get to?
Travellers Cheques
When?
1.3
Count down from 20 to 1.
Food: Say six things you can eat.
5.2
What's the time?
3.1
VISA
Singapore
13254- 0091
VISA
Ireland
7609- 7869 109
1.1
Say the alphabet.
6.2
What's the matter?
What?
4.2
Clothes: Name six things you can wear.
8.3
What are you doing this weekend?
30
9.2
What's the past of ... ?
Where?
Sydney

Student B Activities

Unit 1 Lesson 3

3

	A	B
 Farmers		
 Birds		
 Footballers		
 Cats		
 Doctors		
 Police officers		

Unit 8 Lesson 1

4

__________ __________ Pedro and Juan __________ __________ in the mountains. __________ __________ __________ __________ sunny and the mountains __________. They met __________ __________. They met two girls __________ __________ __________ __________ with them.

Unit 9 Lesson 1

4

Unit 1 Lesson 1

Classroom Language

Look

Listen

Write

Fill in

How do you spell that?

Spelling

Alphabet

CAPITAL LETTERS

QWERTYUIOPASDFGHJKLZXCVBNM

small letters

mnbvcxzlkjhgfdsapoiuytrewq

1

Fill in the gaps with CAPITAL LETTERS and small letters to make the alphabet.

A B C D __ F __ __ I J __ __ __ N O __ __ R __ __ __ __ W __ __ __.

a __ c __ __ __ g __ __ __ k __ __ __ __ p __ __ s __ __ v __ __ y __.

2

Write these words in alphabetical order.

from	hello	you	how	sorry
meet	spell	I	are	where

______ ______ ______ ______ ______

______ ______ ______ ______ ______

Language Summary

***to be* questions**

*Where **am I** from?*

*Where **are you** from?*

*Where **are we** from?*

*Where **are they** from?*

*Where**'s he** from?*

*Where**'s she** from?*

*Where**'s it** from?*

3

What are they saying?

1 Where *am* *I* from?

2 Where ______ ______ ______

3 ______ ______ ______ ______

4 ______ ______ ______ ______

5 ______ ______ ______ ______

6 ______ ______ ______ ______

7 ______ ______ ______ ______

Vocabulary

4

Countries

What are these countries?

1 pgeyt *Egypt*	2 diian ______
3 altiy ______	4 ndaaac ______
5 lednagn ______	6 eeecgr ______
7 najpa ______	8 ncefra ______

5

What does Fernanda say?

Sorry?
Pleased to meet you.
Hello.
Where are you from?
I'm Fernanda Lopez.
How do you spell that?

Hello.	Hello.
______	I'm Akiri Saito.
______	S–A–I–T–O.
______	Pleased to meet you.
______	Japan.
______	Japan.

Classroom Language

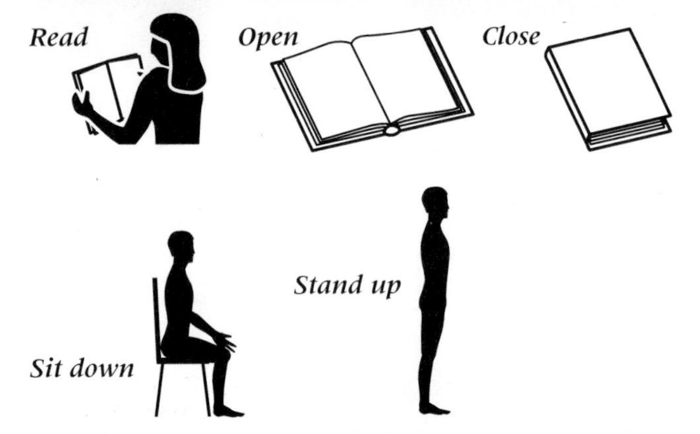

Vocabulary

1

Family

Complete the pairs.

1 mother and *father*
2 grandfather and ______
3 sister and ______
4 granddaughter and ______
5 husband and ______
6 son and ______

2

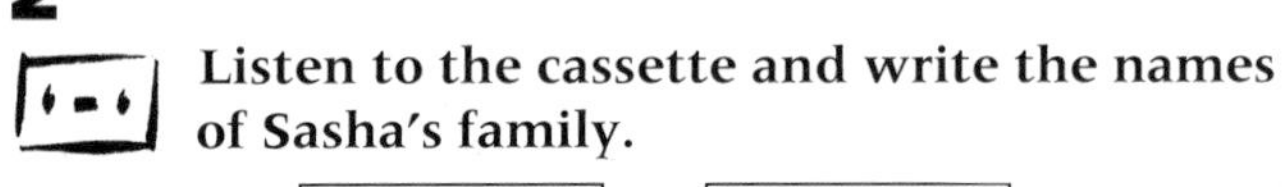

Listen to the cassette and write the names of Sasha's family.

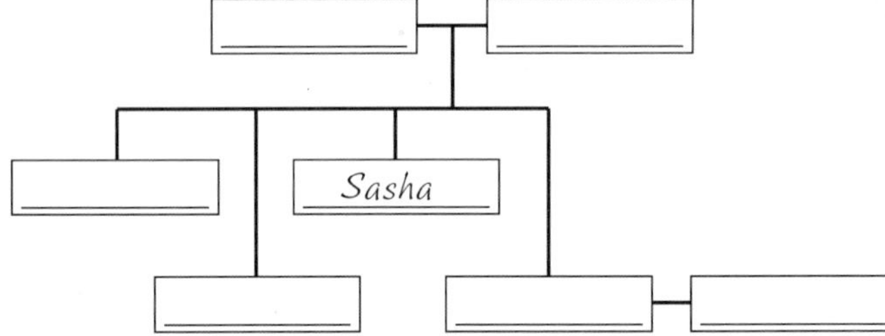

3

The family

Find eight words from this lesson.

A	B	D	S	O	N	M	Q
G	R	A	N	D	S	O	N
H	O	U	V	M	I	T	F
S	T	G	O	Z	S	H	A
T	H	H	M	P	T	E	T
F	E	T	I	D	E	R	H
X	R	E	T	C	R	U	E
P	A	R	E	N	T	S	R

Language Summary

to be		Possessives	
I'm (= I am)		*I*	*My*
You're (= You are)		*You*	*Your*
He's (= He is)		*He*	*His*
She's (= She is)	*from Korea.*	*She*	*Her*
It's (= It is)		*It*	*Its*
We're (= We are)		*We*	*Our*
They're (= They are)		*They*	*Their*

4

Answer the questions.

1 Who's Emma? *She's* Peter's *sister*
2 Who's Alex? ______ Kate's ______
3 Who's Diana? ______ Kevin's ______
4 Who are Peter and Emma? ______ Kate's ______
5 Who's Henry? ______ Alex's ______
6 Who are Kate and Alex? ______ Kevin's ______

Now write about yourself.

I'm ______'s ______ I'm ______'s ______
I'm ______'s ______ I'm ______'s ______

Vocabulary

5

Numbers

Write the numbers.

1 2 + 3 = *five*
2 9 − 2 = ______
3 3 × 3 = ______
4 6 ÷ 2 = ______
5 4 + 2 = ______
6 10 − 2 = ______
7 8 ÷ 2 = ______
8 5 × 2 = ______
9 7 − 5 = ______

6

Days of the week

Write the days of the week.

Monday ______ ______ ______
______ ______ Sunday

Pronunciation

7

Listen and repeat.

/ð/

mo**th**er fa**th**er bro**th**er **th**e

Unit 1 Lesson 3

Classroom Language

Double s

Match

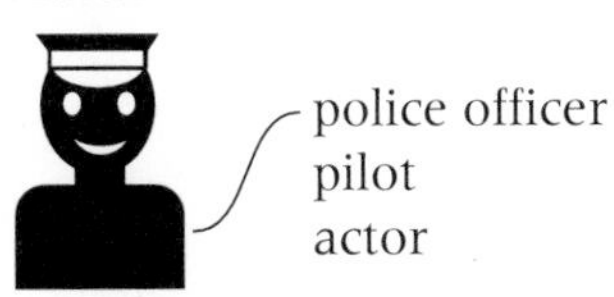

Vocabulary

1

Jobs

Listen and write the words.

1 *student* 2 ______ 3 ______ 4 ______

5 ______ 6 ______ 7 ______ 8 ______

2

Listen and repeat.

Language Summary

a, an, -s

a

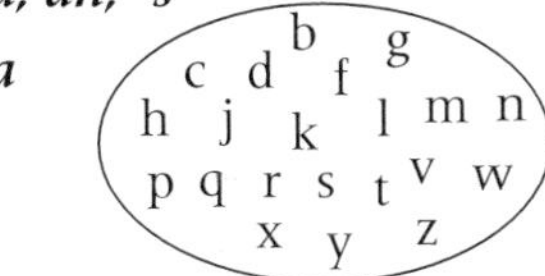

an

a e i o u

*she's **a** doctor*
*he's **a** pilot*

*he's **an** actor*
*she's **an** engineer*

~~*a, an*~~, (___ *s*)

they're pilots, they're actors

*he's **a** business**man**, they're business**men***

3

Correct the mistakes.

1 He's farmer. *He's a farmer.*
2 What you do? ____________
3 where's Anna from? ____________
4 Im Claudio Costa. ____________
5 He's a actor. ____________
6 He's a businesman. ____________
7 Are you an police officer? ____________
8 She's engineer. ____________
9 They're a taxi drivers. ____________

4

Write the questions.

1 *What's your name?* Anna Bright.
2 ____________ A–N–N–A B–R–I–G–H–T.
3 ____________ Australia.
4 ____________ I'm a pilot.
5 ____________ Yes, I've got one brother and two sisters.
6 ____________ It's Tuesday.

Pronunciation

One teacher, two teacher**s** **/z/**

One student, two student**s** **/s/**

/-fs/, /-ks/, /-ps/, /-ts/

5

/s/ or /z/?

1 actors */z/*
2 engineers / /
3 pilots / /
4 footballers / /
5 doctors / /
6 shop assistants / /
7 police officers / /

Listen and check.

6

Listen and repeat.

/ə/

a housewife **an** act**o**r farm**er**s p**o**lice

Unit 2 Lesson 1

Classroom Language

How do you say this?

Language Summary

What's *Sydney* ***like?***
it

It's *beautiful and it's hot in summer.*

1

Listen and fill in the gaps.

Rome is a (1) __________ city. It's the capital of Italy and it's on the River Tiber. It has many (2) __________, (3) __________ buildings, (4) __________ restaurants and (5) __________ shops. It's (6) __________ in summer, and it's very (7) __________ and (8) __________.

2

Think of five places you know. Write their names.

big __________

small __________

quiet __________

busy __________

beautiful __________

3

Write about one of the places from Exercise 2.

____

____

____

____

____

____

____

____

Language Summary

Numbers 0, 11–20

0 zero	*11 eleven*	*12 twelve*
13 thirteen	*14 fourteen*	*15 fifteen*
16 sixteen	*17 seventeen*	*18 eighteen*
19 nineteen	*20 twenty*	

4

What's the number?

1 two four six eight ten *twelve*
2 five seven nine __________
3 twenty nineteen eighteen __________
4 four eight twelve __________
5 one two three five eight __________
6 five ten fifteen __________
7 six four two __________

Pronunciation

5

How many syllables in these words?

1 syllable *3*
2 dangerous ______
3 noisy ______
4 beautiful ______
5 cold ______
6 quiet ______
7 busy ______

6

Listen and repeat.

/w/
where **wh**en **w**et

/ɪ/
b**i**g f**i**fteen S**i**ngapore

Classroom language

Can you say that again?

Language summary

Prepositions

Where's the bank?

It's ***next to*** *the hotel.*

It's ***opposite*** *the café.*

It's ***between*** *the hotel and the bookshop.*

It's ***in front of*** *the cinema.*

It's ***behind*** *the railway station.*

It's ***near*** *the bus stop.*

1

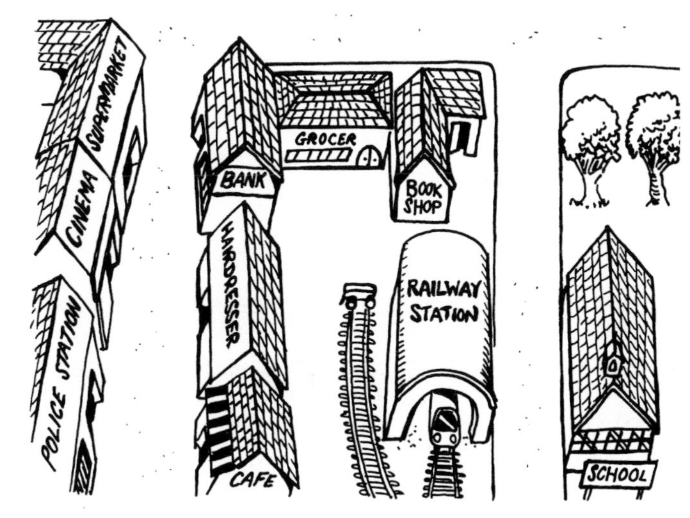

Fill in the gaps.

1 Where's the bank? It's *opposite* the supermarket.
2 Where's the hotel? It's ________ the post office.
3 Where's the hairdresser? It's ________ the bank and the café.
4 Where's the bus-stop? It's ________ the hotel.
5 Where's the hairdresser? It's ________ the railway station.

Language Summary

Giving directions

Turn left. Turn right. Go straight on. Go past *the station.*

2

Look at the map in the Exercise 1. Where are you? Listen and write.

1 *hotel*
2 ____________
3 ____________
4 ____________

3

Write about two places in your town. Use *turn right, turn left, go straight on, go past.*

From ____________ to ____________

____

____

____

____

____

____

____

Pronunciation

4

Syllables

Which word is different?

1 bank school (bookshop)
2 bookshop hotel hospital
3 post office railway station hairdresser
4 police station post office supermarket
5 cinema hospital school

5

Listen and repeat.

/p/	**/e/**
past the **p**ost office	l**e**ft hot**e**l n**e**xt
police station	

Classroom language

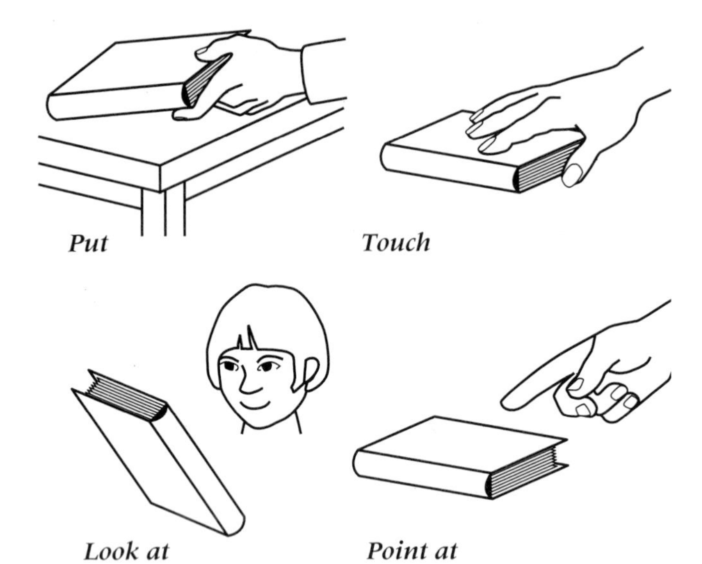

Vocabulary

1

What is there in Danny's flat?

1 aofs *sofa*
2 acritun ________
3 ebd ________
4 degirf ________
5 wohrse ________
6 ondiww ________
7 albet ________
8 knis ________
9 ittelo ________
10 errowbad ________
11 arihc ________
12 itlonivees ________
13 ansbi ________
14 hitlg ________
15 rokeco ________

Language Summary

Prepositions of place

in, on, on the left, on the right, in the middle

2

Fill in the gaps. Use these words:

on the left   in   on   in front of   between   next to

Danny's flat is clean and quiet. There's a sink *in front of* the window. There is a television ________ the table and a chair ________ the table and the sofa. ________ of the door there's a bed. There's a wardrobe ________ the bed. There's a shower ________ the bathroom.

3

Write about your room.

____
____
____
____
____
____
____
____

Pronunciation

4

Word stress

Put the words in the right columns.

■▪	▪■	■▪▪
sofa	*hotel*	*cinema*

doctor   hospital   ~~hotel~~   Brazil   dangerous
Japan   curtains   cooker   ~~sofa~~   Amazon
quiet   beautiful   ~~cinema~~

5

Listen and repeat.

/f/
flower **f**ridge **f**loor

/æ/
c**a**t b**a**nk **A**mazon

Classroom language

Ask

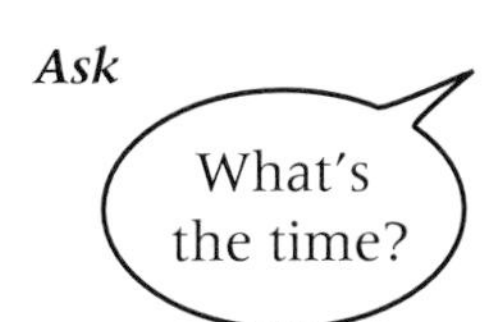

Answer

1

Write the numbers. Find the answers in the line.

1 49 – 9 = *forty* 2 23 + 4 = ______
3 30 + 20 = ______ 4 23 – 21 = ______
5 31 – 9 = ______ 6 5 × 6 = ______
7 4 × 12 = ______ 8 58 ÷ 2 = ______
9 45 – 6 = ______ 10 35 + 15 = ______

forty-eighttwofifty/forty/twenty-seven/fifty/
thirty-ninethirtytwenty-twotwenty-nine

2

Listen and tick the number plates you hear.

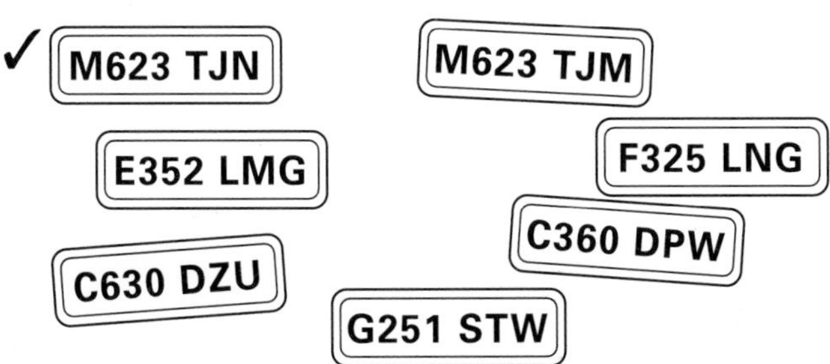

Language summary

Telling the time

What time is it?

It's three o'clock. ***It's seven twenty.***

3

Match the times.

1 five o'clock a 6.10
2 eight fifteen b 5.30
3 seven fifty c 8.15
4 five thirty d 1.30
5 nine twenty e 9.20
6 eight forty f 12.45
7 eleven o'clock g 5.00
8 twelve forty–five h 4.35
9 four thirty–five i 8.40
10 six ten j 7.50
11 one thirty k 11.00

Listen and repeat.

4

Draw the times.

1 four o'clock

2 seven thirty

3 nine fifteen

4 ten forty-five

5 eleven fifty

6 twelve twenty

Language summary

Present simple questions

*What time **does** the supermarket close?*

*What time **do** banks open?*

5

Tourist Information June 1st – 7th

Welcome to Saffron Walden

BANKS: Lloyds 12 King Street hours 9.30–5.00
Barclays The Market Square hours 9.30–5.15
POST OFFICE 32 High Street hours 9.00–5.00
THE CHEMIST Market Square hours 8.30–5.30
closed Wednesday 1.00

CINEMAS
MGM, West Street The Hunchback of Notre Dame
hours 1.30, 4.45, 6.30
ODEON, South Street Independence Day
hours 4.45, 7.30, 9.00

Write the questions.

1 **A:** *How many cinemas are there?*
B: There are two. MGM and Odeon.

2 **A:** ______?
B: At 9.30.

3 **A:** ______ on Wednesday?
B: At 1.00.

4 **A:** ______?
B: At 5.00.

5 **A:** ______?
B: At 5.15.

6 **A:** ______?
B: In South Street.

Pronunciation

6

Listen and repeat.

/θ/ /i:/
thirty **th**ree thr**ee** Kor**ea**

Unit 3 Lesson 2

Classroom language

Circle 

1

How much is it? Listen and circle.

1	£4	£5	($4)
2	£30	£13	£3
3	$66	$56	$65
4	£50	£20.50	£12.50
5	$40	$40.14	$14.40
6	£59.50	£50.59	£15.50

2

Questions

Put these words in the right order to make questions.

1 it is much how *How much is it?*

2 the when train leave does ______________________

3 nights many want do how you ______________________

4 I room see can please the ______________________

5 all right that is ______________________

6 your I can name please have ______________________

Pronunciation

4

Sentence stress

Listen and say these sentences with the correct stress.

Two singles to London, please.

When does the train leave?

I'd like a double room, please.

Can I see the room?

How much is it?

5

Listen and repeat.

/h/	/ʌ/
how much **h**ello	b**u**s d**ou**ble

Vocabulary

3

Transport

Match the words with the pictures.

1 bicycle [c]

2 boat [ ]

3 bus [ ]

4 car [ ]

5 helicopter [ ]

6 motorcycle [ ]

7 plane [ ]

8 train [ ]

a b c d e f g h

Classroom language

1

Match the pictures with the words.

1 Tick ☐
2 Open ☐
3 Fill in ☐
4 Look *c*
5 Read ☐
6 Listen ☐
7 Write ☐

a b c d e f g

2

Write these words in alphabetical order.

1 hairdresser hospital cinema bank post office
bank cinema hairdresser hospital post office

2 two six nine eight one three
____

3 hotel room single double night key
____

4 boat car plane bicycle helicopter train
____

 **Listen and check.**

3

Write five sentences.

My	sister's father's husband's mother's wife's brother's friend's	name is ______ car number is ______ from ______ telephone number is ______ address is ______

My brother's name is Eduardo.
____
____
____
____
____

4

Write the words that should start with a CAPITAL letter.

1 monday cold australia mother beautiful dirty
Monday, Australia

2 bank grandson two switzerland john hot
____

3 paris autumn noisy april train thursday
____

4 anna spring name hotel june bedroom
____

Language summary

have got

I *You* *We* *They*	***'ve got*** *(have got)*	*three sisters.*
He *She*	***'s got*** *(has got)*	
I *You* *We* *They*	***haven't got*** *(have not got)*	*any brothers.*
He *She*	***hasn't got*** *(has not got)*	

5

How many brothers and sisters have you got?

Write about you, your family and your friends.

My mother hasn't got any sisters.
____
____
____
____
____
____

Pronunciation

6

 **Listen and repeat.**

/ɒ/

g**o**t h**o**t tom**o**rrow

Unit 4 Lesson 1

Classroom language

Point at

Vocabulary

1

Clothes

Finish these words.

1 sh _i_ _r_ _t_
2 sw _ _ _ _ _
3 je _ _ _
4 tr _ _ _ _ _ _
5 sk _ _ _
6 dr _ _ _
7 ja _ _ _ _
8 co _ _
9 so _ _ _

2

Clothes and colours

What colour are Tariq's clothes?

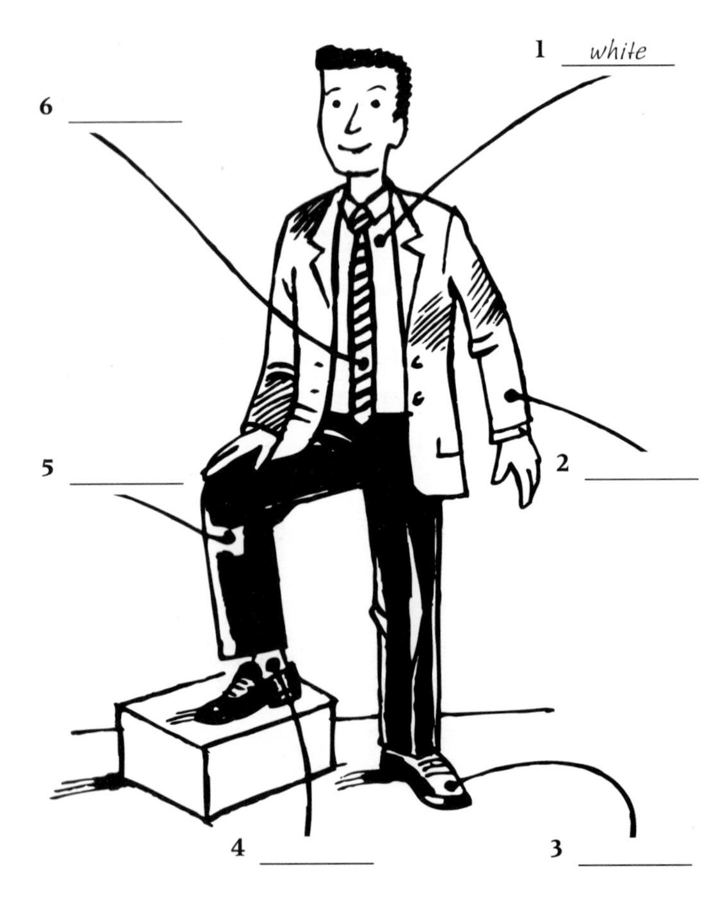

Tariq is wearing a white shirt, a red and blue tie, a grey jacket, black trousers, green socks and purple shoes.

3

What colour are *your* clothes?

I am wearing ______________________

____

Write about someone you know.

____

4

Answer the questions.

1 What colour is your bedroom? ______
2 What colour is the door of your house? ______
3 What colours are in your country's flag?  ______
4 What colour is your classroom? ______
5 What colour are the taxis in your town? ______
6 What colour are your teacher's shoes? ______

5

Fill in the missing telephone numbers.

1 500255 five double 0 two *double five*
2 56213 five six two ______
3 22651 double two six ______
4 999 nine ______
5 426 8190 four two six eight one ______
6 192 one ______

Pronunciation

6

 **Listen and repeat.**

/ʃ/	/ɜː/
shirt **sh**oe	sk**ir**t sh**ir**t

Vocabulary

1
Crossword

Language summary 1

***can* for requests**
***Can I** try it on?*
***Can I** help you?*

2
Write the dialogues for each picture. Use these phrases

Yes. What size?
~~Hello. I'd like a room please.~~
Yes, of course.
Here you are.
Can I see the room?
Double please. How much is it?
Single or double?
Small, please.
Yes please. Have you got this in black?
$60 per night.
Can I help you?

1

2

	1		2
A:	*Hello. I'd like a room please.*	A:	______
B:	______	B:	______
A:	______	A:	______
B:	______	B:	______
A:	______	A:	______
B:	______		

Listen and check.

Language summary 2

It's too …
It's **too** small.

3

1 It's too *big*
2 It's too ______
3 It's too ______
4 It's too ______
5 It's too ______

Pronunciation

4

Listen and repeat.

/k/	/aɪ/
can **c**olour	**I** tr**y**

Unit 4 Lesson 3

1

Circle the word that is different.

1 watch, earring, tie, football
2 magazine, book, camera, newspaper
3 shirt, football, tennis racquet, computer game
4 T-shirt, sweater, shoes, shirt
5 sofa, shower, toilet, bath
6 pilot, actor, brother, farmer
7 father, grandmother, sister, aunt
8 chemist, bookshop, supermarket, school
9 train, boat, bus, car
10 put, in, next to, in front of

2

How much is it? Match the objects to the price

£95.99
£40.30
£14.30
£19.99
£75
£7.50
£2.50
£25
£3.05

Language summary

going to

What	*am I* *are you* *are we* *are they* *is he* *is she*	*going to* take?
I'm *You're* *We're* *They're* *He's* *She's*	*going to* take a camera.	

3

The Rodriguez family are going on holiday. What are they going to take?

Mrs Rodriguez is going to take a ______________________
Mrs Rodriguez ______________________
Lucia ______________________
Lucia ______________________
Mr Rodriguez ______________________
Mr Rodriguez ______________________
Tony ______________________
Tony ______________________

What are you going to take on holiday?

I'm going ______________________

____

____

____

Pronunciation

4

Listen and repeat.

/b/

book **b**ottle **b**rown

Unit 5 Lesson 1

1

Circle the word that is different.

1 coffee (cheese) water tea
2 carrots mushrooms oranges potatoes
3 eggs bread pasta rice
4 fish milk yoghurt cheese
5 breakfast dinner prawns lunch

Language Summary

Present simple

I/You/We/They	*like/love/hate*	*rice./oranges.*
He/She/It	*likes/loves/hates*	

Do you like *rice?*	***Do you like*** *oranges?*
Yes. ***I love*** *it.*	*Yes.* ***I love*** *them.*
Yes, ***I do.***	*Yes,* ***I do.***
It's *OK.*	***They're*** *OK.*
No, ***I don't.***	*No,* ***I don't.***
No. ***I hate*** *it.*	*No.* ***I hate*** *them.*

2

What food do you like?

I like ____________________

I love ____________________

I hate ____________________

3

Look at this table.

I/You/We/They	*like*
He/She/It	*likes*

Write five sentences about your family.

eg My father hates yoghurt.
My mother loves fish. My sister likes bananas.

____

____

____

____

____

4

Listen to Antonio talking about eating in Argentina and Tuti talking about eating in Indonesia. Fill in the grid.

	Antonio	**Tuti**
What time does he/she have breakfast?		
What does he/she have for breakfast?		
What time does he/she have lunch?		
What time does he/she have dinner?		

5

What are you going to have for dinner tonight? (Use your dictionary).

____

____

____

____

____

Pronunciation

6

Listen and repeat.

/l/	/eɪ/
like love lunch	potato train hate

Unit 5 Lesson 2

Spelling

one tomato   *two tomat**oes***
potato   *potat**oes***

1
Write sentences about four dishes you like.

eg *For pizza you need flour, tomatoes and cheese.*
For sukiyaki you need beef, mushrooms and rice.

For __________ you need __________, __________, and __________.
For __________ you need __________, __________, and __________.
For ______________________________
For ______________________________

Language summary

Countable and uncountable nouns

*Have you got any **mushrooms**?* *Yes, but I need **them**.*
*Have you got any **cheese**?* *Yes, but I need **it**.*

2
Put the foods from Lessons 1 and 2 into two groups.

It	Them
lamb milk rice	tomatoes prawns onions
______________.	______________.
______________.	______________.
______________.	______________.
______________.	______________.
______________.	______________.

3
You will hear seven of the words from Exercise 2. Number the words you hear from 1 – 7, and underline the stressed syllable.

1 coffee

4
It or them?

1 Have you got any cheese? Yes, but I need ______.
2 Have you got any spices? Yes, but I need ______.
3 Have you got any mushrooms? Yes, but I need ______.
4 Have you got any bread? Yes, but I need ______.
5 Have you got any tomatoes? Yes, but I need ______.

5

Hello. I'm Helen and I'm from Scotland. I'm a policewoman and I love my job. I love the weekends too. I play tennis. I don't eat meat. I like vegetables and cheese. I love fruit and I drink milk.

Answer the questions about Helen.

1 Where does Helen live? *Scotland*
2 What is Helen's job? __________
3 Does Helen like her job? __________
4 Does Helen eat meat? __________
5 Does Helen drink coffee? __________

Now write about yourself.

____
____
____
____
____

Pronunciation

6
-s

Put these words into three groups.

/z/	/s/	/ɪz/
prawns	carrots	oranges

eggs socks spices mushrooms jackets
dresses bananas skirts lunches trousers
hats shoes ties coats jeans sweaters

Listen and check.

7
Listen and repeat.

/əʊ/

tomat**o** potat**o**es cl**o**thes

1

Listen and tick what Serdar orders.

Big Burger Take-away

Cheeseburger	£2.50	☐
Big Burger Special	£2.75	☐
Lamb Kebab	£3.00	☐
Pizza: mushroom / prawn / four cheeses		
small	£2.00	☐
medium	£2.50	☐
large	£3.00	☐
Green Salad	£1.25	☐
Tomato Salad	£1.50	☐
French fries	£0.90	☐
Drinks		
Cola	£1.00	☐
Tea	£0.80	☐
Coffee	£0.90	☐

Language summary

Would like

I'd like *spring rolls, please.*

Would you like *anything to drink?*

I'll have

I'll have *an ice cream, please.*

2

Fill in the dialogue to buy the food and drink on the table.

1 _Good_ evening.

2 A table ______ two, please.

3 ______ you ready to order?

4 Yes, I'll ______ ______ samosas and ______ ______ ______, please.

5 ______ you like anything else?

6 I'd ______ ______ ice cream and ______ ______.

7 Just coffee ______ me, please.

8 ______ I have the bill, please?

Pronunciation

3

Sentence stress

Listen and repeat.

1 Good evening.

2 A table for four, please.

3 I'll have paëlla and salad.

4 Can I have the bill, please?

5 Just coffee for me, please.

Listen and underline the stressed words.

6 Here you are.

7 A beer and a cola, please.

8 I'd like steak, please.

9 Would you like anything to drink?

10 Can I have a pizza, please?

4

Listen and repeat.

/m/

medium **m**ushrooms **m**ilk

Unit 6 Lesson 1

Vocabulary

1

Parts of the body

Find twelve words in the square.

N	X	T	Y	K	D	O	T	O	E
M	S	T	O	M	A	C	H	P	L
B	C	H	E	S	T	H	U	X	U
B	K	F	O	O	T	E	M	F	Y
H	A	I	R	U	V	E	B	I	F
W	Q	C	G	H	L	K	Z	N	T
H	D	O	K	A	B	D	M	G	E
E	P	Z	H	Y	S	L	E	E	V
I	K	N	E	E	Q	C	A	R	M

Language summary

Comparison of adjectives

Pedro is tall. Zoya is ***taller than*** *Pedro.*

tall	*tall-er*
large	*large-r*
big	*big-ger*
noisy	*nois~~y~~-ier*

2

Look at the picture and write sentences about Andrea and Sarah. Use these words:

~~old~~ ~~light~~ tall long short young dark

1 *Andrea is older than Sarah.*

2 *Sarah's hair is lighter than Andrea's.*

3 ______

4 ______

5 ______

6 ______

7 ______

3

Write five sentences about your family or friends.

My sister is taller than my brother.

______

______

______

______

______

4

Match the pictures with the sentences.

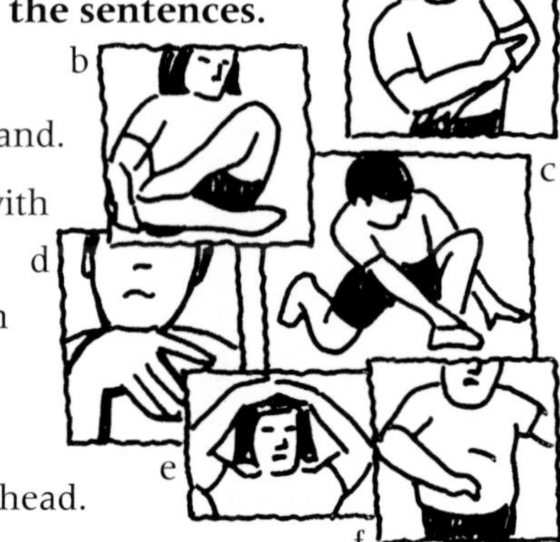

1 Point to your stomach.

2 Put your chin on your hand.

3 Touch your right knee with your left foot.

4 Touch your left foot with your right hand.

5 Point to your elbow.

6 Put your hands on your head.

5

Write sentences for these pictures.

1 Touch your left knee ______.

2 ______.

3 ______.

4 ______.

Pronunciation

6

Listen and repeat.

/t/	/d/	/ɔː/
tall **t**ea	**d**ark **d**rink	tall sh**or**t

Unit 6 Lesson 2

Language summary

Present simple negative

I *You* *We* *They*	*don't*	*feel very well.*
He *She* *It*	*doesn't*	

1

Make a dialogue. Put the words in the correct order.

1 how you are?
How are you?

2 very I feel don't well.
____

3 Oh dear. the matter what's?
____

4 throat got I've sore a.
____

5 doctor think see you a I should.
____

2

Correct these sentences.

1 I've got cough. *I've got a cough.*
2 You should to go to bed. ____________________
3 What the matter? ____________________
4 I'm not feel very well. ____________________
5 My shoulder hurt. ____________________
6 I've got footache. ____________________

Language summary

should

I *You* *He* *She* *It* *We* *They*	*should*	*go to bed.*

3

Write sentences giving advice to Alexander.

1 *You should*
2 ____________________
3 ____________________
4 ____________________
5 ____________________

4

What's the matter? Listen and write.

1 *She's got a headache.*
2 ____________________
3 ____________________
4 ____________________
5 ____________________

Pronunciation

5

Listen and repeat.

/g/
got **g**o

/ʊ/
sh**ou**ld g**oo**d f**oo**t

Unit 6 Lesson 3

Vocabulary

1

Add five words to each list.

1 purple, yellow, green *blue* ____ ____ ____ ____

2 socks, dress, tie ____ ____ ____ ____ ____

3 chemist, department store, sports shop ____ ____ ____ ____ ____

4 chocolate, tomato, salad ____ ____ ____ ____ ____

5 quiche, paëlla, pizza ____ ____ ____ ____ ____

6 elbow, eyebrow, hair ____ ____ ____ ____ ____

7 long, tall, big ____ ____ ____ ____ ____

8 cough, backache, flu ____ ____ ____ ____ ____

2

Write the words in the puzzle. What is number 15?

1 *r*	*a*	*i*	*n*	*b*	*o*	15 *w*							
					2								
				3									
		4											
			5										
					6								
						7							
					8								
						9							
						10							
				11									
			12										
						13							
						14							

3

Dictation

Listen and write.

1 *What's the matter?*

2 ____

3 ____

4 ____

5 ____

6 ____

Pronunciation

4

Listen and repeat.

/r/	/u:/
rainbow **r**ose	bl**ue** t**oo**

Unit 7 Lesson 1

Language summary

Telling the time

*8.30 = **half past** eight* *8.45 = **a quarter to** nine*

*9.20 = **twenty past** nine*

Present simple for daily routines

I *You* *We* *They*	*wake up*	*at seven o'clock.*
He *She* *It*	*wakes up*	

1

When do you get up? Write sentences about your day. Use these words:

wake up get up have breakfast go to work/school have lunch go home go to bed

1 *I wake up at* ____________________
2 ____________________
3 ____________________
4 ____________________
5 ____________________
6 ____________________
7 ____________________

2

Read about Carsten's Sunday. Number the pictures in the correct order.

On Sunday Carsten gets up at ten o'clock and reads the newspaper in bed. He has bread, cheese and coffee for breakfast, and then he goes to the park and plays football with his friends. Then he goes home and has a shower. At two o'clock he has lunch in a restaurant with his parents. In the afternoon he watches football on TV. In the evening he meets his girlfriend and goes to the disco.

3

What does Ellie ask Carsten? Put the words in order to make questions.

Ellie: Sunday time What do get you up on ?
What time do you get up on Sunday?

Carsten: ten o'clock.

Ellie: you breakfast What do have for ?
____

Carsten: Coffee, cheese and bread.

Ellie: morning you in do the What do ?
____

Carsten: I play football in the park.

Ellie: do lunch When have you ?
____

Carsten: At two o'clock.

Ellie: with Who lunch you do have ?
____

Carsten: My parents.

Ellie: you afternoon What do do in the ?
____

Carsten: I watch football on TV.

4

Ask someone the questions in Exercise 3. Write about his/her Sunday.

____
____
____
____
____
____
____

Pronunciation

5

 **Listen and repeat.**

/v/ have lunch T.V.

/ɑː/ half past

Unit 7 Lesson 2

1

Write the words and match them with the pictures.

1 aregnid ______________ [6]

2 nigmismw ______________ [ ]

3 okigocn ______________ [ ]

4 ynglif ______________ [ ]

5 nurignn ______________ [ ]

6 nadnigc ______________ [ ]

Language Summary

like + -*ing*

*I **like** reading.*

*Do you **like** swimming?*

***I quite like** it.*

***She really likes** it.*

*I **don't like** dancing.*

2

What do Helen and Jacques like? Listen and write 'Helen' or 'Jacques' in the correct column.

	really likes	quite likes	doesn't like
watching TV			*Helen*
playing computer games			
playing volleyball			
reading			

3

Write sentences about Helen and Jacques.

Helen really likes reading.

____

4

Write these sentences correctly.

1 I likes running. *I like running.*

2 We love go to the gym. ______________

3 They doesn't like travelling. ______________

4 Do she like watching TV? ______________

5 He likes really playing volleyball. ______________

6 Does you like cooking? ______________

5

Read about Lucian and Estelle and write the questions.

Lucian and Estelle are from Nice, but they live in Paris. They work for Renault, the car factory. Lucian and Estelle like swimming and cooking. They don't have a car. They don't like driving!

1 live/they/do/Nice? *Do they live in Nice?*

2 Paris/do/live/they? ______________

3 Ferrari/they/work/do? ______________

4 work/Renault/do/they? ______________

5 swimming/like/cooking/they/do? ______________

6 swimming/they/like/travelling/do? ______________

7 like/do/driving/they? ______________

Pronunciation

6

Listen and repeat.

/ŋ/ sleep**ing** sin**g**er wro**ng**

/aʊ/ h**ou**se m**ou**th

Unit 7 Lesson 3

Vocabulary

1

Languages

Look at the languages. Write the countries and underline the stress.

Countries	Languages
England	English
______	French
______	Spanish
______	Japanese
______	Greek
______	Italian
______	Turkish
______	Portuguese
______	German
______	Chinese
______	Russian

Language summary

***can** for ability*

		can	
I/You/He/She/It/We/They		***can't** (cannot)*	*swim.*
Can	*I/you/he/she/it/we/they*	*swim?*	
Yes,	*I/you/he/she/it/we/they*	***can**.*	
No,	*I/you/he/she/it/we/they*	***can't**. (cannot)*	

2

Manda would like to sail round the world. Listen to her job interview and answer the questions.

1 Can Manda sail? *Yes, she can.*
2 Can she swim? ______
3 Can she cook? ______
4 Can she speak Spanish? ______

True or false?

5 Her mother's got a boat. ______
6 She can't sail very well. ______
7 She swims every day. ______
8 Her family quite like her cooking. ______
9 She has Spanish lessons every week. ______

3

Can or can't? Listen and write.

1 *can't*
2 ______
3 ______
4 ______
5 ______
6 ______
7 ______
8 ______
9 ______
10 ______

Language summary

Adverbs of manner

*He's **a good singer**. He **sings well**.*
*She's **a bad singer**. She **sings badly**.*

Adjectives	Adverbs
bad	*bad**ly***
dangerous	*dangerous**ly***
good	***well***
fast	***fast***

4

Write five sentences about yourself, your family and your friends. Use these words.

play ~~drive~~ cook talk swim run

well badly beautifully noisily quietly slowly fast safely dangerously

My father drives dangerously.
______
______
______
______
______

Pronunciation

5

Listen and repeat.

/n/

can no nose

Language Summary

was, were

*What **was** the weather like? It **was** hot.*

*What **were** the people like? They **were** friendly.*

1

Read this holiday advertisement.

Marina is a beautiful, quiet island. The beaches are clean and the sea safe and the weather is hot and sunny. Hotel Nirvana is on the beach and it's got two big swimming pools. There are three restaurants with friendly waiters and very good food.

Winona would like to go on holiday to Marina. Petra and Rudi went there last year. Petra liked it but Rudi hated it. What did they say to Winona? Use these words:

clean	hot	on the beach	big	
beautiful	good	friendly	sunny	quiet

It was *beautiful.*

The weather ____________ The beach ____________

The hotel ____________ The waiters ____________

It wasn't *quiet.*

The beach ______ ______ The weather ______ ______

The swimming pools ______ ______ The food ______ ______

Language Summary

Past simple

Present/Infinitive	**Past**
go	***went***
buy	***bought***
drink	***drank***
eat	***ate***
meet	***met***
sunbathe	*sunbathe**d***
dance	*dance**d***

*Where **did** they **go**?*

*They **went** to the mountains.*

*They **didn't go** to the beach.*

2

Read the text. Write the questions below about Tamsin's holiday.

Last September Tamsin went to Bali. She went by plane and stayed in a big hotel. It was very hot, so she swam every day. In the evenings she went to different restaurants – the food was very good. She met some nice people and every night she danced with them at the disco. She was happy because she wasn't alone.

1 *Where did she go?* Bali.
2 ____________ Last September.
3 ____________ By plane.
4 ____________ In a big hotel.
5 ____________ It was very hot.
6 ____________ She swam.
7 ____________ It was very good.
8 ____________ Some nice people.

3

Answer four questions you wrote in Exercise 2 about your last holiday.

1 ____________
2 ____________
3 ____________
4 ____________

Pronunciation

4

Listen and repeat.

/j/

your **y**esterday **y**es

Unit 8 Lesson 2

Language Summary

Past simple

He bought two tickets to Hawaii.

Present/Infinitive	**Past**
phone	*phone**d***
pack	*pack**ed***
open	*open**ed***
lock	*lock**ed***
drive	***drove***
say	***said***
break	***broke***
hear	***heard***
sing	***sang***
take	***took***

Pronunciation

1

-ed

Put these past tense verbs in the right columns.

went packed swam ate stayed
had met started sunbathed locked
drank called bought did climbed drove
said wanted broke sang took finished
phoned opened looked visited

/d/	**/t/**	**/Id/**	**irregular**
stayed	packed	started	went

Listen and check.

2

Here are some more irregular verbs. Match the present and the past forms.

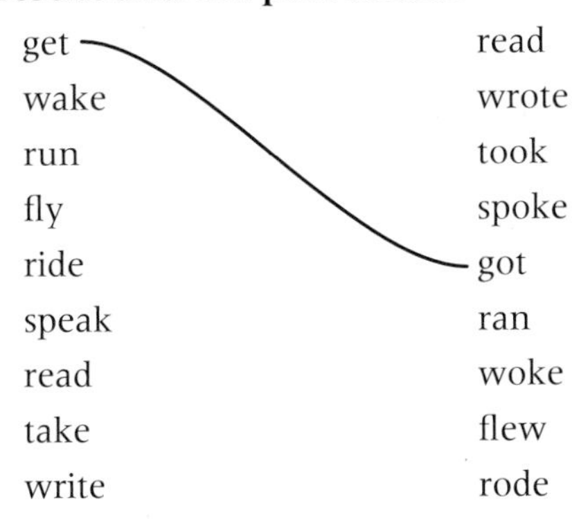

get	read
wake	wrote
run	took
fly	spoke
ride	got
speak	ran
read	woke
take	flew
write	rode

3

Listen and write.

(1) ___Last___ Monday, Mr Angelos (2) ________ ________ ________ travel agent (3) ________ bought two airline tickets. (4) ________ Tuesday, Mr (5) ________ Mrs Angelos packed (6) ________ suitcases, locked (7) ________ front door (8) ________ ________ goodbye (9) ________ ________ neighbour.

(10) ________ Wednesday (11) ________ burglar (12) ________ into (13) ________ flat. (14) ________ opened (15) ________ desk (16) ________ took (17) ________ money. Then (18) ________ ate (19) ________ ________ ________ food (20) ________ drank (21) ________ ________ ________ champagne.

Listen again. Practise reading the story.

Language summary

Joining sentences

He played the piano. He sang a song. He had a bath.
He played the piano ***and*** *sang a song.* ***Then*** *he had a bath.*

4

Read about Anya. Number the pictures in the correct order.

Tommy is Anya's husband. He gave her £1,000 to pay for a holiday. She took the money to the supermarket (1) ________ went shopping. She put the money in the trolley (2) ________ put the shopping on it. (3) ________ she walked to her car (4) ________ put the shopping into it. (5) ________ she drove home. She left the money in the trolley!

Use *and* or *then* to fill the gaps in Anya's story.

Pronunciation

5

Listen and repeat.

/t/	/d/	/Id/
lock**ed** pack**ed**	open**ed** call**ed**	want**ed** visit**ed**

Vocabulary

1

Months

Find twelve months of the year in the square.

S	E	P	T	F	E	B	C	R	S	T
E	L	D	D	E	C	E	M	B	E	R
P	A	U	E	B	I	M	M	A	U	N
T	W	A	J	R	S	A	A	P	N	J
E	J	A	N	U	A	R	Y	R	I	U
M	U	U	R	A	N	C	F	I	J	L
B	G	G	L	R	O	H	L	L	U	Y
E	R	U	V	Y	A	P	R	S	N	S
R	O	S	N	O	V	E	M	B	E	R
O	C	T	O	B	E	R	U	N	E	N

Language summary

Times in the past

I saw him **last night**.

When did you last have a haircut? **Three weeks ago.**

yesterday

last night
week
month
year

the day before yesterday

the night before last
week
month
year

three days ago
weeks
months
years

2

When was ...

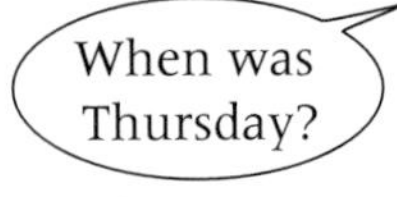

Today is Saturday, so Thursday was two days ago.

1 Thursday? ______________________

2 June? ______________________

3 1990? ______________________

4 Saturday? ______________________

5 1996? ______________________

6 December? ______________________

7 Your birthday? ______________________

8 Your last holiday? ______________________

3

Match the questions with the answers.

1 When did you learn to drive a car?
2 What did you watch on television last night?
3 What did you do last weekend?
4 Who were you with at 4pm today?
5 When was the beginning of term?
6 How did you come to class?
7 What did you eat for breakfast this morning?
8 What was the month before last?

a By bus.
b The news.
c 6th September.
d On Saturday I played tennis and on Sunday I slept.
e January.
f Three years ago.
g John.
h Toast and coffee.

Now answer the questions for yourself.

4

Complete the story. Use the verbs in the brackets.

Last year I (go) (1) *went* on holiday. I (drive) (2) __________ to the sea with my friend. On the first day we (look) (3) __________ at the beautiful buildings and (eat) (4) __________ in lots of restaurants. The next day (be) (5) __________ very hot so we (drive) (6) __________ to the sea. We (leave) (7) __________ our clothes in the car and (sunbathe) (8) __________ and (swim) (9) __________ all day. At six o'clock we (walk) (10) __________ to our car, but the car (be) (11) __________ there. We (buy) (12) __________ some clothes and (go) (13) __________ to the Police Station. The police (be) (14) __________ nice and we (sleep) (15) __________ in the police station.

Pronunciation

5

Listen and repeat.

/dʒ/
June **j**azz **j**acket

/tʃ/
Mar**ch** wat**ch** **ch**icken

Unit 9 Lesson 1

1

Listen and write down these phone numbers.

1 *01799 52291*
2 ______
3 ______
4 ______
5 ______
6 ______
7 ______

2

Put this conversation in the right order.

_____ **B:** No, it's OK. I'll call back later.
_____ **A:** I'm sorry. He's not here. Can I take a message?
_____ **B:** Bye.
_____ **B:** Hello. Can I speak to Abdullah, please?
1 **A:** Hello?
_____ **A:** OK. Bye.

Listen and check your answers.
Practise the conversation with a partner.

3

What's the weather like? Write the sentences under the right pictures.

It's raining. It's snowing. ~~It's sunny.~~
It's cloudy. It's windy.

It's sunny ______ ______

______ ______

Language summary

Present continuous

What	*am I*	*doing?*	*I'm*	*reading.*
	are you		*You're*	
	are we		*We're*	
	are they		*They're*	
	is he		*He's*	
	is she		*She's*	

4

What are the people doing? Look at the picture on page 66 and write five sentences.

A man is having a bath.

______
______
______
______
______

Spelling

5

Put the words in the right column.

~~play~~ ~~type~~ cook run walk come sail
have sleep drive shop travel fly skate

read/reading	dance/dancing	swim/swimming
play/playing	*type/typing*	

Pronunciation

6

Listen and repeat.

/ʒ/
televi**s**ion

Vocabulary

1

Entertainment

What shall we do this evening? Find ten words in the square.

C	O	M	E	D	Y	L	R	O
H	L	S	I	R	P	L	A	Y
I	J	A	Z	Z	O	T	C	R
N	O	O	S	I	P	E	B	O
E	E	R	T	S	L	W	F	C
S	N	I	N	D	I	A	N	K
E	G	M	U	S	I	C	A	L
C	A	R	L	O	D	C	A	N
T	H	E	A	T	R	E	S	L

Language summary

Making suggestions

Shall we *go to the theatre?* ***Let's*** *go to the cinema.*

Saying what you want

I'd rather *go to the disco.*

2

Listen and correct these sentences.

1 Abigail has two tickets for ~~the theatre~~. a concert
2 Frank is free on Saturday. ______
3 Abigail and Frank are going to a club. ______
4 They are meeting at 7.30. ______

Pronunciation

3

Intonation

Listen and fill in the gaps.

1 a Shall we go to the Chinese restaurant?
b Yes. 

2 a Let's go ______
b Yes.

3 a Why don't ______ this afternoon?
b Yes. 

4 a What about ______
b Yes.

5 a Let's go ______ 
b Yes.

6 a Shall we ______ 
b Yes.

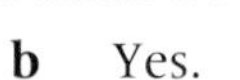

Listen again and fill in the faces.

4

Albina and Mia are in Paris. What does Mia say?

Pronunciation

5

Listen and repeat.

/eə/

h**ai**r ch**ai**r

Unit 9 Lesson 3

Language Summary 1

Prepositions of time

at four o'clock	***in*** the evening	***on*** Monday
at the weekend	***in*** the morning	***on*** Tuesday evening

1

Fill in the gaps.

I have a lot to do this week because I'm going on holiday (1) *at* the weekend. I'm seeing Chigusa (2)______ Wednesday – we're going to a concert (3)______ the evening. My mother's coming to take the dog (4)______ Thursday morning, and (5)______ the afternoon I'm going shopping for clothes. I'm finishing work (6)______ three o'clock (7)______ Friday so that I can get to the airport on time.

I'll send you a postcard!

Love, Bianca.

Present continuous for future arrangements

Language summary 2

I'm seeing *my mother at 8.30 tonight.*

2

What is Clara doing next week?

Monday *12.30 Doctor*	Friday *4.45 Hairdresser* *7.30 Cinema with Zoë*
Tuesday *phone Zoë*	Saturday *11.30 meet Jane*
Wednesday *1.15 Lunch with Mum*	Sunday *6.00 Tennis with Jon*
Thursday	

1 *On Monday she's going to the doctor at 12.30.*
2 ______
3 ______
4 ______
5 ______
6 ______
7 ______

Language Summary 3

Making suggestions

Would you like to *have dinner with me?*

What about *Thursday?*

3

Write the sentences in the right order.

Joe: I tonight can you see ?
Can I see you tonight?

Clara: sorry seeing I'm brother my
______

Joe: Saturday doing what on you are ?
______

Clara: morning the going in hairdresser I'm the to
______

Joe: lunch OK like to you would have ?
______

Clara: time great what ?
______

Joe: one o'clock.

Where is Clara going with Joe?
______

Dictation

4

Listen and write.

1 *What are you doing tonight?*
2 ______
3 ______
4 ______
5 ______
6 ______
7 ______

Pronunciation

5

Listen and repeat.

/ɪə/

ear here

Unit 10 Lesson 1

Vocabulary

1

Write the dates.

1 3.8.81 _3rd August 1981_
2 21.2.75 ________
3 23.3.68 ________
4 6.4.71 ________
5 1.8.94 ________
6 30.11.83 ________

2

Write the questions and answer them.

1 what you wearing are? _What are you wearing?_
I'm wearing black trousers and a white shirt.
2 sitting who next you are to? ________
____
3 going where are tonight you? ________
____
4 sitting you are where? ________
____
5 it snowing is? ________
____

3

Read the text and answer the questions.

Abraham Lincoln became President of the United States of America for the first time in 1860. When he was young he lived in a log cabin and his family did not have much money. He did not go to school so he worked very hard, and read a lot of books at home. Lincoln was tall and thin, and he was kind. He liked people and people liked him.

He became President again in 1864. On April 14, 1865 Lincoln went to the theatre with his wife. An actor saw Lincoln, got a gun and shot him. He died the next day.

True or false?

1 Lincoln was president for one year. _F_
2 Lincoln started school in 1860. ______
3 He lived in a log cabin. ______
4 Lincoln read a lot of books at school. ______
5 He was a tall man. ______
6 He was very friendly. ______
7 An actor shot Lincoln and his wife. ______

4

Listen and complete.

He ______ ______ but he ______ ______ America. He ______ ______ ______ ______ ______ and ______ .
He ______ ______ ______ friends. His ______ ______ ______ Yoko. A ______ ______ ______ ______ ______.

Who was he? ________

Pronunciation

5

Listen and repeat.

/ɔɪ/

b**oy** s**oy**a sauce

1

Fill in the gaps with these prepositions.

for in ~~to~~ for by in with in next

Last summer we went (1) *to* Sweden (2)______ a holiday. We went (3)______ boat. We stayed (4)______ my uncle and aunt (5)______ their house (6)______ to the sea. Everyday we swam (7)______ the sea and went for walks. We stayed (8)______ Sweden (9)______ two weeks and it was wonderful.

2

Match A and B.

	A	B
1	fly	a boat
2	swim	a bicycle
3	drive	an aeroplane
4	ride	in the sea
5	row	a bus

3

Match the sentences with the correct speech bubbles.

I'd rather buy this one.

I'd like a coffee please.

How much is the chocolate?

I'd like a single to London please.

Let's buy this game.

Is this the train to York?

Can I see your ticket, please?

So do I

Can I help you?

I like thrillers.

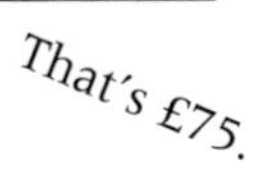

Pronunciation

4

Circle the odd word out.

1 /fɪʃ/ /hɔ:s/ (/bɔɪ/) /bɜ:d/

2 /vɑ:z/ /tʃeə/ /teɪbl/ /trɪ:/

3 /nəʊz/ /bæg/ /leg/ /ɪə/

4 /tenɪs/ /seɪlɪŋ/ /fʊtbɔ:l/ /kəmpju:tə/

 **Listen and check.**

1

Answer these questions.

1 Where were you at 7.30 this morning?

___

2 Where were you at ten o'clock last night?

___

3 Where were you yesterday morning?

___

4 Where were you this time last weekend?

___

5 Where were you three days ago?

___

Ask a friend the questions. Write the answers.

1 ___
2 ___
3 ___
4 ___
5 ___

2

Find a word from the book for each letter.

A *pril*	S ___
C ___	T ___
C ___	A ___
E ___	R ___
L ___	T ___
E ___	E ___
R ___	R ___
A ___	
T ___	
E ___	

3

Put these words in the correct category.

July scarf boat T-shirt arm sofa coat chair curtains rice knee lamb wardrobe chocolate train ~~carrots~~ March stomach bicycle cupboard neck bus January jacket feet mushrooms September sweatshirt May aeroplane

food	clothes	transport
carrots		

furniture	parts of the body	months

Add three more items to each list.

4

Write about yourself, your family, your interests, what you do every day, your favourite things.

___

5

Look back at the book and answer these questions.

1 Where does Anna come from? *Australia*

2 What three letters of the alphabet sound the same as A? ___

3 Kevin is Henry's grandson. Who is Alex? ___

4 What's the job? RENIEGNE ___

5 What time do people have dinner in Spain? ___

6 What food do you need to make Sukiyaki? ___

7 Which is wetter? London or Chicago? ___

8 What are the colours of the rainbow? ___

9 Who went to Hawaii? ___